Writing Workshop in the Elementary Classroom

Writing Workshop in the Elementary Classroom

A Practical Guide for Teachers

Kathleen Puente
Jenny C. Wilson

ROWMAN & LITTLEFIELD
Lanham • Boulder • New York • London

Published by Rowman & Littlefield
An imprint of The Rowman & Littlefield Publishing Group, Inc.
4501 Forbes Boulevard, Suite 200, Lanham, Maryland 20706
www.rowman.com

Unit A, Whitacre Mews, 26-34 Stannary Street, London SE11 4AB

British Library Cataloguing in Publication Information Available

Library of Congress Cataloging-in-Publication Data Available

Names: Puente, Kathleen, 1960–, author. | Wilson, Jenny C., 1976–, author.
Title: Writing workshop in the elementary classroom : a practical guide for teachers / Kathleen Puente, Jenny C. Wilson.
Description: Lanham : Rowman & Littlefield, [2019] | Includes bibliographical references.
Identifiers: LCCN 2018036265 (print) | LCCN 2018046494 (ebook) | ISBN 9781475847147 (electronic) | ISBN 9781475847123 | ISBN 9781475847123 (cloth : alk. paper) | ISBN 9781475847130¬ (paperback : alk. paper)
Subjects: LCSH: English language—Composition and exercises—Study and teaching (Elementary). | Language arts (Elementary)
Classification: LCC LB1576 (ebook) | LCC LB1576 .P84 2019 (print) | DDC 372.62/3—dc23
LC record available at https://lccn.loc.gov/2018036265

Printed in the United States of America

To all my students, who helped me learn that writing helps us to find ourselves in the most ordinary events of our lives.

—Kathy Puente

—◦◦◦—

To the students who remind me that they are brighter writers and thinkers than we often give them credit for. Specifically, Sydney, Jae, Kelsey, Steven, and Dekeitra, who still remind me of my growth as you grew as writers.

—Jenny C. Wilson

Contents

Introduction   ix

Part I: The Structure of Writing Workshop   **1**

  1 Nonnegotiables   3

  2 The Writing Process   11

  3 Collecting Topics   17

  4 Organizing   23

  5 Drafting   31

  6 Revision Conferences   37

  7 Revision Draft   47

  8 Editing Conference   51

  9 Edited Draft   63

 10 Publishing Conference   67

 11 Publishing   77

 12 Sharing   81

Part II: Putting It All Together   **87**

 13 Mini-Lessons and Mentor Texts   89

 14 Teacher Conferences   107

 15 Peer Conferences   117

 16 Student Notebooks   121

17 Collecting Data   127

18 Managing Papers   133

19 Grading   137

20 A Schedule for the First Ten Days   141

21 Writer Development by Grade   145

Conclusion   159

References   161

About the Authors   163

Introduction

It seems that every introductory education class has an assignment to decide if teaching is art or science. We both had to choose between the two as if someone had asked whether breakfast was eggs or bacon. We have reflected on this question many times over the years and have always come to the same conclusion: teaching cannot be described simply as one or the other but instead exists on a sliding scale, moving between science and art as needed.

Teaching is using the science of learning to artfully engage students in their quest for knowledge. Teachers can possess vast amounts of content knowledge, but unless they draw students into an engaging dance, this content will at best be learned only on a superficial level. Leading students through the surface skills of sentence structure, correct punctuation, precise spelling, and other often-tested conventions of writing to a deeper struggle with purpose, soul, and voice lies at the art of teaching writing, and in this space writing becomes owned by its writer and not the teacher, the test, or the classroom.

Many students hate writing and do not hesitate to communicate this to their teachers. They will expound on how boring it is and how they have nothing to write about, but the opposite is true.

About six weeks into Kathy's first year of experience with writing workshop, she told the class to put away their math books and get out their writing folders. She got applause . . . yes, applause! We usually receive satisfaction in our job through our students' learning, not through appreciation for a job well done, so you can imagine her delight with the clapping and cheering because the students knew they were about to write.

She thought maybe this class was unusual, but at about the six-week mark something wonderful always seemed to happen surrounding writing in class. She had no fireworks, nor did she offer them food or money. Instead, the students wrote each day for forty-five minutes, moving through the writing process at their own pace and conferring with Kathy and their peers to help refine their pieces with the end goal of sharing with an audience. Accolades such as these can only mean that students were fully engaged in the quest to write and learn about writing, and it is from those experiences that we write this book.

We hope you find your students engaging with writing in the same way. Writing workshop offers no tricks. It does provide a framework for students to move systematically through the writing process as they find their voice and their own reason to write. It's not magic. But the end result is magical as students engage in the struggle to communicate in deep, sometimes profound ways.

THE STRUCTURE OF THE BOOK

Our writing workshop is different than traditional ways of teaching writing, such as using prompts or correcting sentences, and thus it creates a need to reimagine your teaching and your classroom. In this text, each chapter centers on one aspect of writing workshop, showing why that aspect is important and how it can be used with the amazing things you already are doing. This book takes special issue with curriculums centered on prompts, testing, and other barriers to real writing.

At the end of each chapter you will be asked to think about how you would organize each particular aspect of writing workshop in your own class. Although parts of writing workshop are essential, the details surrounding the essentials are flexible in ways that allow you to design the workshop to run smoothly in your classroom for your style of teaching and your students' style of learning. To make writing workshop happen in your classroom involves choosing how you interact with students as well as managing the flow of students, papers, and workload.

When you reach the end of this book, you will have a complete plan and be ready to teach writing workshop in your own classroom. The notion that it is your space, although a bit redundant, is profound. As increasingly outsiders are said to know how to "turn someone or something around," we take the distinct stance that the power lies in the teacher.

The two sections in this book give you the information and structure you need as well as ideas on how to make writing workshop work through all of the requirements, curriculum, and standardized tests. Part I journeys with you through the structure of writing workshop and the parts of the writing process as they apply to the workshop. Many educators throw around the term *writing workshop*, using it synonymously with *writing process*. The two terms are closely connected but distinct concepts. They will be clarified in this section.

Part II of this book shows how to work with and manage peripheral aspects of conducting writing workshop in your class. In a classroom, a teacher ties together the content, pedagogy, and management of the student body to bring about a learning structure. The content is set by the standards and time lines your state or district puts forth. Writing workshop provides the structure to teach the content in meaningful ways that align with the goals classrooms need to measure success and those that teachers know make students better writers.

Managing the students, the time, the physical space of the classroom, and the supplies will be integral to beginning writing workshop and making it run smoothly. Attending to these peripherals enables a space for students with different abilities, beliefs, and experiences to create learning and writing spaces with their teachers.

THE PLANNING JOURNAL

Teachers design the flow of the learning activity and facilitate the learning, but teachers are not the center of learning. The students are the learners, and therefore, are the center of a good lesson. Learners need direction and information to move forward; then, they need time to wrestle with the content in ways that bring success.

This book is written for teachers as learners. To give you time to approach this new content in real ways, a topic is provided for you at the end of each section to use as a planning journal. You will need a journal to write down your personal plan and your mentor text as you move through this book. Because writing workshop is a structure in which to teach writing, many decisions fall to you as you work through this book so the structure fits your style, your classroom, and your students. The planning journal will help you engage with that and keep a record of your thoughts.

Writing workshop is a multifaceted way to teach writers. Much of it is one-on-one and is differentiation in its highest form, moving each student forward at his own pace and within the developmental writing stage from which he enters. Writing workshop may seem difficult to carry out as it moves away from traditional instruction where a prompt is assigned and everyone writes on the same topic with specific parameters (such as twenty-six lines, three high vocabulary words, or even memorizing a prewritten piece for use on a test).

Conversely, writing workshop explains how to handle the differentiated moving parts that is simpler once you have a good solid plan. When you work out the details, writing workshop will give you the power to teach your students as they grow in their writing ability and with more joy, eagerness, success, and ease. Yes, ease.

As you move from your plan into the teaching of writing through the workshop, you will change things that aren't working; and you will continue to make changes each year, as methods and plans need tweaking with each new group of students. Change is a continual part of writing workshop as your students become better writers and you become a better teacher of writing. Take time to plan each part. The journaling in this book will help you to do that, to question yourself and others, and to think about being a teacher of writers. When you put writing workshop into practice, your students will develop as writers in a world in need of good communicators.

HIGH-STAKES TESTING: THE ELEPHANT IN THE ROOM

High-stakes testing is part of education in the United States and cannot be ignored; however, it does not have to take over instruction. Politicians and the media tell the public that high-stakes tests will hold teachers accountable and improve schools, but often they have the opposite effect. Teachers have a huge need to be good at their jobs, and many times we feel that high test scores show that we are good at our jobs. This produces test-centric instruction (instruction focused on one high-stakes test such as Common Core or STAAR) so our schools get the sole outcome they want—high scores—visible when teachers try to find the shortest distance to correct test answers from instruction. This high-stakes mind-set creates teachers stuck in a place where the world of a child is equivalent to a test score. When this happens, teachers are left with the sense that something is wrong with those struggling in their classes, labels for those children, and worse, behavior issues as children lose deep instructional time devoted to their needs and strengths.

Teachers fear that their professional decision-making ability about instruction might not be good enough or translate into good test scores in a system where instruction that looks much like the high-stakes test score—not learning—is valued and often even reinforced. Although scores are important, they are not the reason we teach, of course.

Writing instruction that involves a prompt and a set number of lines is teaching to the test. This kind of writing does not take into account all of the types of writing people do in real life. It boxes in writing and creates a one-size-fits-all genre where the writer's thoughts are robotic, stilted, and constructed with forced adjectives.

Students hate this kind of writing. It makes them write about things that have no meaning in their lives. It makes them write in ways that go against the natural communication they use daily. Writing becomes drudgery for the teacher and for the students when it is so disconnected from real uses. Students do not want to write, and teachers do not want to grade twenty-five papers with the same constructed composition they felt forced to assign.

When young students learn the craft of writing through authentic writing, they become good writers, and good writers always pass the test. Because writing workshop focuses on the individual needs at the moment students need instruction, personal growth can be gained. Contrast a writing classroom in which lessons are taught and grammar is attempted on premade sentences to writing workshop, in which writing structures are taught within the students' own structures; lessons are particular to the needs of the class and the individuals. Therefore, the better the writer, the stronger the chance she will pass the test. So, the logic for teaching authentic writing overpowers any logic that uses the path of formulaic writing to create better test scores. If formulaic writing worked to create original, well-written essays, engaging children with literacy would not be a struggle. But it is. The remedy is for students to write authentically, with support.

When students write authentically, they come to love writing. They look forward to writing class. They think about what they will write next even when they aren't in school. They become engaged and involved in writing as they take ownership of what they write and how they write. The most important product of writing authentically is a student who writes well.

The goal is to design a plan that works in your classroom with your students, wherein writing is something personal to be shared. Students will make meaning through their writing and translate it into better writing; in turn, that will translate into better writing scores. Be strong in your professionalism. Give it a try, and you will be pleased with the results. It sounds too good to be true, but it isn't.

This book provides an easy-to-read text that works through process writing so teachers can to begin as soon as they want. They can work through the book at their own pace and as they finish it, have ready-made ideas and plans for their writing instruction. Most books concerning writing workshop develop a process that is complicated and hard to insert into the classroom, especially if the school year has begun already. This is why many teachers do not engage in writing workshop: it seems too difficult to install in their classroom. Many books use multiple folders and composition books, handouts and difficult passages. This book is meant to be easy to read and follow: the whole purpose is for teachers to begin wherever they are—and meet the children wherever they are.

Part I

The Structure of Writing Workshop

This first section of the book explains the concept and framework of writing workshop. Chapters 1 and 2 describe the structure of the workshop and the writing process. Chapters 3–12 talk about the parts of the writing process in detail, explaining what the students and teacher are doing for each part. At the end of part I, you will have a plan for taking students through the writing process and conferring with them.

DEVELOPING A MENTOR TEXT

In any writing class, teachers are the best writers (Gallagher, 2011). No matter how gifted a student may be as a writer, you are better because you have more experience and more education. Oftentimes as teachers we forget this! Use your expertise as the best writer in the class to model writing. From collecting topics all the way through sharing a finished piece of writing, you need to demonstrate a good writing model to your students as they attempt the process of writing.

At the end of each chapter, you will be asked to plan how you will execute each aspect of the writing process in your classroom. You also will be given the opportunity to develop a piece of writing to use as a mentor text. Take the time to produce this mentor text to use during mini-lessons. This might seem like something to do later, but it isn't.

Because students need to see how writers produce a good piece of writing, have one you will work through at each interval, showing students the struggles, errors, changes, conferences, revisions, and edits that go into making a good piece of writing. Do not create a perfect piece of writing for each step, but rather produce mistakes on purpose (and naturally) so you can think aloud with students when you use it as a teaching tool. Students need to hear metacognitive talk in order to develop their own metacognitive talk as they write.

Writing is problem-solving, so modeling that problem-solving will help students solve their own writing problems and become better writers. Through your example, students will acquire a similar clearer mind-set about the goal of writing, and they will know that they have support as they are writing. Good writers are made, not born.

Chapter One

Nonnegotiables

Although writing workshop is moldable to your style and the level of your students, the structure of writing workshop is nonnegotiable. To see real growth in writing, writing workshop must occur every day, consistently, and with form and function. Children need routine and structure, yet they like spontaneity and trying new things. Writing workshop gives students all of these things by providing the structure each day and freedom within the structure to communicate their thoughts and experiences through text.

The teacher designs the routine and the structure but provides for spontaneity and freedom to try new things. Students grow in their writing ability with writing workshop because they write every day and receive the instruction they need at that time. It also provides that scaffolding when they need it.

Lessons are not done to remedy some skill in a whole-class structure. Instead, lessons showcase expectations of good writing and writers in ways that then can be expected in student writing. Growth happens incrementally, not in big spurts; therefore, writing needs to happen consistently to make incremental growth become longtime, usable learning. Setting up this structure so it can happen every day is necessary for success with writing workshop. Find the time; talk to your administrators if there doesn't seem to be time.

THE STRUCTURE OF WRITING WORKSHOP

- Mini Lesson (5–10 minutes)

- Status of the Class (1–2 minutes)
- Writing and Conferencing (20–40 minutes)
- Sharing (5–10 minutes)

Many teachers use a writing process to teach writing, but if it is not in the above structure, it is not writing workshop. Writing workshop follows this structure so that students learn something new through direct teaching, have a large amount of time to work on a piece of their choosing, have conferenced help from a knowledgeable individual, and have a chance to share with their peers every day. That structure proclaims the doing of writing as the most important part of becoming a writer. Writers who don't write and don't receive help when they need it, at the developmental level they need it, have little chance of becoming quality writers.

We encourage you to try it. Be faithful to this process for at least six weeks. Make writing workshop time sacred. It can be done with as little as thirty minutes or as long as an hour a day, but it needs to be done consistently. Learning to be a writer happens slowly, day by day. Students become deeply involved in the process over time where more learning and more engagement happen within the process of writing.

Writing workshop time becomes predictable for the students, and they look forward to working on their pieces. They begin to think about their pieces at other times during the day at school and at home, waiting for the time when they can add new ideas to their pieces. Writing each day means that students are thinking about writing in deep and complex ways that bring meaning to their work. When schoolwork has meaning and significance in the lives of young people, they are engaged, just as adults become in engaged in their own work when it has meaning and significance.

Skipping days breaks the routine and the flow for teachers and students. If you have an assembly or a field trip, move writing workshop to another part of the day. Be flexible with your daily schedule, but be rigid about having writing workshop at some point in the day, at least for the first six weeks. The only time you should skip writing workshop is to give a writing benchmark test. When teachers have said that writing workshop doesn't work for them, we look back at the issues: it always comes down an inconsistent schedule. If writing is not important to the teacher, it will hold no importance for students either.

When writing is not consistent, forgetfulness about the next step, disconnection to the topic, and even general malaise about the piece can be common, not only for you but for students. If you have students who want to change a topic often or cannot remember what to write, they don't necessarily need a graphic organizer. Instead, they need time on their topic and connection to their writing. When writers are connected daily, boredom is infrequent.

All of your teaching about writing will be done at this time. Everything you need to teach about the craft of writing will be included in writing workshop. No other lessons on punctuation, grammar, or spelling are needed. Students will learn from mini-lessons, conferences, hearing others' writing, and engaging in writing every day. Being in the process daily is where learning occurs. Make as much time as you can for writing workshop.

Mini-Lesson

This is a short five- to ten-minute lesson on some aspect of the craft of writing. Here are a few possible topics:

- process
- conventions
- spelling strategies
- grammar
- capitalization
- apostrophes
- nouns
- verbs
- past tense
- proper nouns
- sentences
- making a good lead
- structuring a good ending
- drafting
- revision
- peer conferencing
- publishing
- reading a piece
- commenting on someone else's piece

Really, a mini-lesson can be on anything that involves the writing craft and is within the scope and sequence of your curriculum. Such a running list as we just provided could easily come from your scope and sequence or district curriculum. It can be tailored for your class, a student, or the needs of your team.

The mini-lesson is an introduction to a new concept or a reminder of a previously introduced concept. It is a quick, clear explanation on how something works in the process of writing. The teacher shows, and the students listen. Guided practice and independent practice come in the writing and conferencing because it is embedded practice. Students learn by writing and discussing their writing with another writer, whether a teacher or peer.

Mini-lessons give students the information they need to try new ideas and concepts in their writing. The mini-lesson is a suggestion for experimenting with new ideas and concepts.

A mini-lesson is short and to the point, taking no more than ten minutes' class time. If you find yourself spending more than ten minutes, you are talking too much. When you are talking, students are not writing. Thus, shorten your talk and have them write to ensure that they understand the concept, knowledge, or skill. You present the information in the mini-lesson; then, check their writing during conferences to see if they are using the concept or convention correctly. Holding yourself to ten minutes will help you hone your skill in presenting information quickly that students will understand easily. The key words for mini-lessons are *concise* and *precise*.

Be aware that just because students don't always use a capital letter doesn't mean they haven't been taught when and how to use one. A teacher should know the age and development of her students: when something is a review and might have been taught in a prior grade versus a newly taught or difficult task.

For example, capital letters are taught in kindergarten and are expected to be used appropriately by first grade, yet many teachers become exasperated when fourth-grade students still use them incorrectly, or not at all. This is true of periods, something students are shown in kindergarten as they begin to write and expected by first grade. As sentences become more complicated, though, students in fifth grade might struggle with fragments or run-ons. As teachers, we must be aware of objectives set forth by the district and state. This awareness will help you know how long a mini-lesson should be, depending on whether they have seen and experienced the skill. Remember, if one or two students reluctant are struggling with a skill, say capital letters, their editing conferences with you will provide an opportunity to be reminded and scaffolded. Everyone need not be taught again.

Status of the Class

This is a quick check (1–2 minutes) and a list of what students are doing that day. It is a way for students to think about what they did yesterday and where they are today in the process of their pieces. Even more, the status of the class is a way to keep data over time on each student's progress. The data can be used to help you become better at teaching writing, to use when talking to parents or administrators, to stay in touch with each differentiated need, and to keep the students moving along at the right pace.

Writing and Conferring

The bulk of the time in writing workshop is used for student writing and student–teacher conferencing. Learning occurs during writing and conference time—deep and complex learning. Students are engaged in writing—working out what they want to say, structuring sentences, figuring out conventions, choosing the right words, and writing the best piece they can. Once they understand the expectations and process, students become engaged writers. They are *in*! Students write about what they want to write about, they learn to make sense of their world in ways other activities cannot manifest, and they get to talk about their favorite subject—themselves! This makes the activity of writing engaging, reflective, and deep.

In conference is where 90 percent of your teaching happens, though most conferences will last less than five minutes. Conferring is student-specific and differentiated instruction at its finest. As the teacher, you will be looking at a specific piece of writing with the child, helping her improve that piece with exactly what she needs at that time for that piece of writing. The teaching is pertinent, exact, and quick, and it works like no other teaching you've done before.

Conferring will seem difficult at first, but over time you will become good at it. Through the struggle of figuring out what each student needs you will learn the most as a teacher, about yourself and your individual student. It is worth it once you see how effective conferences truly are.

Conferring can seem hard at first because you have to come up with suggestions for the piece on the spot. Writing is dynamic and specific to the writer, so the focus of the conference will be different for each child. Still, you will begin to find patterns in all students' writing that will lead you to ideas for mini-lessons and for conferring with other students. Conferring will become your favorite part of teaching simply because it is so personal and interactive, the very reason many of us became teachers. One comment we often get is how teachers really get to know each student through conferring, making it a wonderful way to enjoy students on a daily basis.

This book will present options and strategies for making the most of your individual conferences with students. It will help you set up structures for classroom management of students and papers. It will give you strategies for keeping conferences to five minutes or less and ideas for keeping track of what was taught during a conference.

Students will begin to monitor their own writing as well. As they do, they will begin to ask questions pertaining to their learning and needs. They will know that writing is about learning over time and trust that their prose will get better through the process because they have a teacher who is interested in their particular needs.

Much work in the classroom is about a future test or a benchmark, not about now. Learning is now in writing workshop, and conferring gives impetus for communicating through words and sentences in a way that connects to other human beings. Conferring also gives students personal agency as they are the ones making the final choices for their piece of writing.

Sharing

Each day one or two students will finish a piece, but the work is not done until the piece has an audience. When students share their writing with the rest of the class, it is one of the most powerful parts of writing workshop. To see a proud student share a piece he has worked so hard on as other students marvel at the words on the page is magical. The purpose for their writing comes forward as they communicate with peers their heartfelt thoughts and meaningful insights into life. Peers are the perfect audience: they are on about the same level, with similar experiences in life and in writing. Having an audience breathes life into a piece.

Sharing gives other students ideas for their writing. Students get ideas on ways to publish, different sentence structures, introductions, conclusions, illustrations, and word choices. We often are surprised at what students carry away from sharing time. When first beginning writing workshop in a class, a teacher might see it as merely a platform for students to engage with an audience, but sharing time gives students ways to compare and contrast others' writing with their own, mentally engaging with texts that can spur ideas and reinforce teaching.

Sharing is the culmination of a piece of writing, but it also signals the beginning of a new piece as the process starts over. The process is the key to learning how to be a good writer, but the consistency of writing and conferring every day propels good writers to write better.

—∕∕∕∕∕—

PLANNING JOURNAL: YOUR THOUGHTS ON THE NONNEGOTIABLES OF WRITING WORKSHOP

This is not a scripted curriculum, so you, the professional, will have to make a lot of choices about how you use writing workshop in your class. Focusing on the three aspects of teaching— content, pedagogy, and management—you will need to decide how to set up the structure and movement of writing workshop throughout the year. Think about who your students are at the beginning of the year and where you would like them to be at the end of the year. Where are the students developmentally? If you teach kindergarten or first grade, starting with pictures and moving through the year toward words would be a goal. If you teach fourth or fifth grade, your goals might be focused on genres and more academic writing (see table 1.1).

Table 1.1.

Name	Date	Goal
Jonathan	8-16-2018	Pictures with one word
	10-19-2018	One sentence with beginning and ending punctuation

The management of writing workshop will call for the most decisions, particularly in the beginning. Running writing workshop effectively is different than traditional lessons in which the teacher is in control all of the time. Writing workshop means you are giving the students autonomy to write what they want and time to work on those pieces. Providing for student autonomy is the hardest part, as teachers are sure that chaos will ensue. Surprisingly, students rise to the occasion over time and write more than you thought possible or had experienced in the past. It just takes a bit of time and teacher perseverance concerning behavior.

As students fall in love with writing, order will be the mainstay; even the occasional student disruption will be handled better because the expectations for this time are very clear. Students will help maintain order because they will be in control of their own writing and the writing space. It will have meaning for them and be important to them. Still, you need to plan for the movement and routines in the class to minimize disruptions. Writing workshop is the avenue that engages the students in the craft of writing; and when students are engaged, learning happens at personal and profound levels.

Now, it's time to put down this book. Get a journal (paper or computer) and begin a plan for how you will teach and manage writing workshop. This is the most important part of learning something new or instantiating something you already knew. Book learning, as you are doing now, only works when it is put into action.

- Start by writing your philosophy on teaching writing. It need not be long, but it should explain how you imagine writing and what being both a good writer and a good writing teacher entails. This will help you keep a focus at the center of all of your writing plans.
- What goals would you like to accomplish during the (remaining) school year?
- The structure of writing workshop is nonnegotiable. What concerns you about this structure? What things can you do to alleviate those concerns?
- Why would allowing students to choose their own topics create better writers?
- How will giving students long periods of time every day to write make better writers?
- Now, what will writer's workshop look like in your classroom? If someone entered, what do you imagine they would they see?

Chapter Two

The Writing Process

Most teachers are familiar with the writing process; however, teachers often equate the writing process with writing workshop. They are not the same. The writing process is a part of writing workshop, but writing workshop encompasses so much more. In many classrooms, the writing process is taught the whole class with all students writing the first draft on the first day, editing the next day, and publishing on the third day.

In writing workshop, students write at their own pace, choosing their own topics, and are guided and facilitated personally by the teacher. This means that everyone is at a different place in the writing process every day depending on factors such as how fast they write, their style, or how long they envision the writing to be. Writing workshop allows students to work through the process at their own pace every time they write a piece.

For teachers this might sound a bit scary, with scattered drafts in different stages; actually, you can feel secure in knowing where each student is, what his strengths are, and what is coming next. The student, in turn, will feel confident because he too knows what happens next and he trusts you to make his piece better. He knows he needs help, and you are helping to ensure that the piece moves forward with the skill and knowledge he needs. It is OK that not everyone is at the same writing stage. Learning is truly differentiated!

Professional writers have a process: planning, drafting, revising many times, getting others to look at it and give feedback, having editors look it over for conventions, and, finally, bringing it to readers. How often a writer revises, what a writer looks for in revisions, and when a writer is ready to share can be very personal and specific. Although we don't have the luxury of multiple revisions when we only write for an hour each day, this process can be mimicked with a few modifications.

For purposes of workshop, there must be a process that gets students writing, teaches them the procedures and conventions, explains how to talk about their writing, and gives them experience about how others write. All the while, students must get into the writing in their own way, at their own pace, and find their own voice. This process will allow all students the learning experiences they need to become good writers. This is what the writing process offers writing workshop. It creates a structure for writing that organizes and substantiates writing over time. The writing *process* is the structure in which the students experience writing; writing *workshop* is the structure in which students learn how to write.

Figure 2.1 shows an example of the writing process for students. Remember, the writing process is what is happening in writing workshop.

Because students are unique, with varying writing abilities, they will not move through the process in the same amount of time. Quick writers will finish a piece in five to six days. Slower writers, or those who have much to say about a story or topic, will finish a piece in ten to twelve days. The finished pieces will not be of the same quality. Accept what the students produce and, through the process, help them make their next pieces a little better than the ones before. Growth happens slowly over time, so continually working through this process creates progress throughout the year. Don't expect a piece to be perfect, just better than it was before, and work for which the child feels accomplishment and pride.

Standards give us a benchmark for how children on average in that grade level should be writing. Some children will hit the mark, some will still be growing toward it, and some will be beyond it. Problems arise when we expect *all* of our students to write at the grade-level standard.

When students fall short of the standard, deficit thinking steps in and stalls progress because we think, "They can't write." Instead, we always need to look at what the students can do and move them forward from that place, even if it is below grade level. The student is doing her best work and can only improve from that place. Accept what the student gives you and nudge her just a little bit toward better writing, whatever that may look like. Help your students grow from where they are to becoming stronger writers.

Writers who write better than the standard often learn the least because what they produce gets good grades. Often, we think those students' writing is the best in the class, so no improvement is needed, and we lose the oppor-

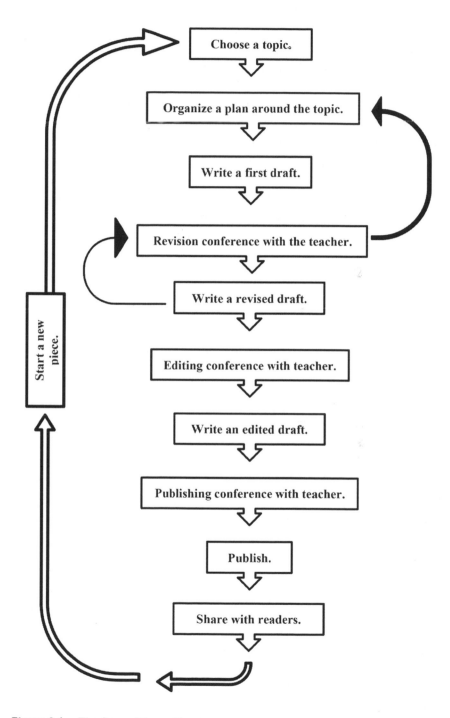

Figure 2.1. The flow of the writing process.

tunity to help these students flourish. Because of this, the good writers in class often are the hardest to teach; we need to think beyond the standard to the student's actual next step in learning. Any writer can improve. This comes from experience with the writing process and instruction from the teacher.

Each part of the writing process couched in writers workshop methodology is integral to the process of becoming a good writer and will be addressed independently in this book. The order of the writing process is not rigid and can be thought of as flexible or fluid. At times a student will need to revise a second time or return to organizing the topic again, but typically, moving through each of these parts is necessary for creating a good piece of writing.

Deep thinking goes on during each stage of the writing process, but the thinking for each part is very different. Organizing the topic requires the writer to focus on the big idea and what she want to communicate to the reader. The writer has to figure out necessary details and where she should go in the piece. This takes a lot of thinking as she moves and shifts the ideas around, finding just the right sequence or grouping of ideas.

Composing the first draft requires putting all of the details into sentences so that they make a coherent piece. Students have to focus on letters, words, and sentences as they develop a flow. At lower grade levels, the students also are focused on forming the letters and the sounds each letter makes as they put their thoughts on paper. Revising requires students to clarify the writing, rearranging thoughts, adding new ideas, and deleting unnecessary ideas. Students will also fuss over word changes to bring just the right cadence and meaning to the piece.

Editing requires thinking about conventions and rules, as the writer works to make the piece reader friendly. Reading it and rereading it with an editor's eye helps make the flow and main points obvious to the reader. Publishing requires students to design page turns and illustrations for sharing with others in ways that showcase the work. Students pay attention to design in ways that help convey meaning to the piece. It is important for students to move through each part for every piece so that learning occurs in constructive ways, and they figure out how writer's work is experienced.

Writing within the structure of the writing process every day will help mediate the students' learning. Breaking it into parts, each with its particular task, and moving through the parts in a specific order brings predictability to the task of writing, which helps give students agency with their work. When they know what to do and when to do it, they can continually focus more attention on improving their writing as they experience writing daily.

———⁓⁓⁓———

PLANNING JOURNAL: YOUR THOUGHTS ON THE WRITING PROCESS

Sectioning the writing process gives specific tasks to writers and helps them focus on the task at hand. This helps writers learn to move through the process with purpose. Write your thoughts on how the writing process will work in your classroom.

- In the writing process, revision is a separate step and comes before editing. Why do you think this is true?
- How might the process differ between your neediest writer and your best writer?
- Create as anchor chart for students to use as a resource.
- What questions do you have at this point? Keep them handy to look for answers as you continue to read.

Chapter Three

Collecting Topics

In writing workshop students choose their own topics. No prompts are given. The biggest fear teachers have as they start writing workshop? That their students will not know what to write about; they will become stuck in the black hole of writer's block. Some teachers have even experienced writer's block. But, in workshop, this is not true. Why? Because everyone's favorite topic is himself.

Students are the center of their own life; their thoughts, feelings, and experiences are always with them and are personal to their truths. So when teachers promote who students are and their interests, having ideas to write about is not a problem.

True, older students may have a harder time if they have spent years writing only to prompts. When students are told what to write about—in prepackaged, shortened, nonconnected ways—they struggle to think on their own, to imagine that their ideas and opinions matter as a writer. After a few good mini-lessons and practice, choosing a topic becomes easier for them.

You want to teach your students this: writing does not have to be about *only* exciting and exotic things. Writing can be about ordinary events and people in their lives—their pets, best friends, a bad haircut, favorite food, hobbies, and sports. It's not what you write about that is important; it's how you write about it.

Writing about their bedroom can become funny when they talk about how the room smells like potato chips. Writing about a bad haircut can be full of emotions, with a sigh of relief at the end that reminds us all that hair does grow back. Writing about the most mundane things becomes interesting when they write the story with a unique perspective. This perspective is what the students can groom and grow with each piece as they improve their writing.

It is helpful to have personal topics to choose from, so collecting topics must be a recurring part of writing workshop. Use mini-lessons to introduce ways of collecting; model thinking about experiences, topics, and ideas that would make good writing topics for your writing. Have students spend a few minutes after the mini-lesson collecting their ideas for writing.

The first day of writing workshop can be about collecting topics, but mini-lessons on collecting can be revisited about once every other month as students gather more ideas and grow as writers. You will find that students will think of ideas outside of writing workshop time and may need reminders to add them to previous collections of ideas.

Create a space for students to collect their ideas in one section of their notebooks so that all of their ideas are in one location and can be accessed easily. If students ever whine that they have nothing to write about, you can redirect them to that collection of ideas. The students definitely will find ideas there because those ideas are their own, and having them handy whenever they are needed will help make writing accessible.

DIFFERENT WAYS TO COLLECT TOPICS

Here are a few ways to collect ideas for writing, but they are not the only ways. Model them in your mini-lesson as part of your writing and as a mentor text for the students. As the most experienced writer in the group, students need to see you think out loud about how to collect topics for writing. Talk about why a topic is important to you and how you might write the piece.

Students should make their own collection right after the mini-lesson. They may include some topics that you have included in your collection because they think it is a good idea. Let them do that, but encourage them to think of things and experiences that are unique to them. They will improve at collecting as the year progresses. These examples are ways to promote thinking about oneself and the world around us. The goal with collecting is to get them to think more readily about their experiences as they navigate their spaces.

What I Like

Begin by drawing a vertical line down the middle of the paper and a horizontal line across the paper. Label the four quadrants:

1. People and Animals
2. Places
3. Things
4. What I like to do: _____

Thinking out loud, write down a few people or animals you like. Leave a few lines blank at the bottom, explaining how you leave room for ideas that come later. Then move to places you've been. These can be faraway travels, but they can also be local places—a hobby store, the local swimming pool, your favorite restaurant, even your kitchen or backyard. Move next to things, inanimate objects you enjoy or that are special to you. Books, movies, or your favorite blanket are good examples. Finally, write down a few activities you like, such as bowling, cooking, writing, or walking your dog. Talk aloud as you gather ideas, allowing students to listen to your thinking. Thinking out loud gives your students a framework for their own thinking.

Heart Map

In her book *Heart Maps: Helping Students Create and Craft Authentic Writing*, Georgia Heard (2016) provides a visual tool to help writers map what is close to their hearts. Draw a large heart the size of the paper. Begin by naming something or someone you love most and jotting it in the middle of the heart. Section it with lines. Continue until you have filled the heart with all of the things you love.

Once you have a bunch of these, your heart will look like a jigsaw puzzle. The items on this list would make a good poem or descriptive piece, but they also can act as topics for heartfelt stories. Getting students to collect and write about topics that are close to their hearts will help give their stories more power through emotions and descriptions. The stories will be deeper with more connections to the reader as they try their hand at these stories from the heart.

Authority List

List things you are an authority on or know a lot about: how to make a particular dish, play a game, or complete a project are a few ideas students can relate to. This shouldn't be a long list, just things you excel at and thus are an "authority" on the topic. This list is good for expository writing.

When students pick a topic from their list, they need to be able to write about it in detail. Sometimes students get really excited about writing a piece about a video game or a sport. Older students do better at these topics because they can remember all of the details that need to be added. Younger students may begin such a piece and soon want to abandon it because it takes too long and frustrates them. Although a younger student can play a video game, writing about the video game takes much more thinking and work than the student may be ready for. Abandoning a piece when this happens is OK, and the student will learn more about his limitations and what it takes to write such a piece. Someday the student's skills will catch up with his interests, and then he will be able to write the piece.

Authority pieces do not always need to be about how to play the game or sport. They can be about why the game is fun to play or the camaraderie that happens from playing a team sport. Steering students toward this focus is a way to match the student's skills with the topic and still retain that air of authority.

Emotional Times

Draw a large circle and section it in six parts like a pizza. On the outside label each section with an emotion such as happy, sad, angry, nervous, silly, and proud. Use more complex words for older children, or add synonyms to words they choose. This allows the larger, Tier 3 words to be shown in context. Then add events in your life where the emotion will be the focus, or the "so what?" of a piece. This will help the students make the emotion the center of the piece as well as bring more depth to the piece. These are great topics for narrative writing as they get to the heart of the story and the purpose of writing about events in the student's experience.

I Want to Know More About . . .

Write a list of topics about which you don't know much but would like to know more. This list can be used for research topics when you teach about research writing or for those who like expository writing. Students will research these topics before they begin writing, and they will need to learn how to read for information, reread for information, use an index, use a table of contents, and take notes. When you are ready to have students collect these topics, plan mini-lessons on the other necessary skills so that research becomes doable. Our experience has shown that when students pick the topic for a research paper, the research process almost teaches itself because the motivation to learn and write about a topic of real interest is huge.

Persuasive Topics

List things you want but will need to convince someone else to get them. This list can contain personal items, such as a new phone; or larger societal quests, such as getting people to drive less to lessen air pollution. Use this list to teach persuasive writing. Getting students to take a stand on a personal or societal issue and then having them argue logically for that point not only makes them better writers, but also makes them savvier when listening to persuasive arguments.

—————

PLANNING JOURNAL: YOUR THOUGHTS ON COLLECTING

Now, it's time to plan how you will teach collecting ideas. Write down your plan with attention to these details:

- Make your own collections by trying each collection idea yourself. You can use these examples as mini-lessons and mentor texts.
- Where will the students keep their collections of ideas? (More on this is in chapter 17.)
- What will be your first mini-lesson on collecting?
- Plan your collecting lessons to coincide with each genre unit. When will the collecting lesson happen within each unit?
- How many collecting lessons will you have during the year? Write a plan.

Chapter Four

Organizing

Once students have chosen a topic, drafting will be easier if they have thought about the details that manifest their topic. Confronting a blank page and beginning to write is really hard, but if students have ideas organized around a topic, composing will be much easier. Writing down ideas and organizing them help students make connections and remember the details that will need to go into the piece of writing. Organizing helps students include all of the information required to make sense of the story or topic and leave out extraneous information. Organizers are tools that students can use to help shape their writing for focus, details, structure, and flow. These are powerful tools in the hands of young writers as organizers help students make sense as they navigate their writing.

Organizers help students compose the first draft. Key to a good organizer is to write just one word or a short phrase for each idea. Students naturally will want to put sentences into the organizer, making it too wordy. An organizer should be laid out so that the writer can see the flow of ideas and how they are grouped. Once the ideas are organized, all the student has to do is make a sentence of each idea. The writing might be bare bones, but it will be set in a good structure that can be revised much easier than a piece that is disorganized. Older students might add a few more details—still, not complete sentences, but more subtopics.

Students learn through many of their reading lessons how the main idea is connected to supporting details. Make a connection to those lessons when teaching organizers that call for a main idea and supporting details. This will help students organize for cohesion, thus improving the structure of their pieces from the start. The type of organizing they will do depends on the genre in which students are writing. In personal narrative, a chronological list of events might be best. If they are writing about someone they know, making subcategories with supporting details will be needed. Students writing an expository piece benefit from writing categories.

The important takeaway for students is that they can organize their thoughts in different ways, but they should choose a method that best fits the type of writing before them. The teacher not only models how to organize a piece, but makes sure students try each method so they know which type of organization will help them most. When students are allowed to choose which way to organize and then do it on their own, the sense of agency produces better results. Students will improve at choosing and using organizational structures over time, which leads to the student autonomy that a teacher wants to promote.

Showing the students different ways to organize is best done in mini-lessons. As you model organizing for a piece of writing, talk about your thought process as you form the structure of a future piece. Modeling metacognitive talk gives students valuable information about the ways in which writers think and organize their thoughts. Then require students to try the organization from the mini-lesson on their next piece to give them experience with that particular organizer.

You can require a separate conference to look over the organizer and help them tweak it, which allows you to do a quick check for understanding and answer any questions they may have. Students may only need these conferences with the first couple of pieces. Once you see that students have the hang of organizing, they can work on their own and move directly into their first draft. If a student seems to have a disorganized first draft, look at the organizer. If the problem lies there, you can help the student reorganize the piece and then rewrite the first draft. Tell that student you want to have a conference after she has planned the organizer for a quick check before she writes the next first draft. Work with the student specifically on organizing until you feel she can do it independently.

As students gain experience with various ways to organize their ideas, they will become very good at it. At times, they may come up with their own ways of organizing a topic. Younger students will have far fewer ideas about how to organize, as their pieces will be much shorter. As with any part of writing workshop, assess where the student is in writing skill development and move forward from that point with an idea of where you eventually would like the student to be.

TYPES OF ORGANIZERS

You can find great graphic organizers online and through writing curriculums, service centers, and your colleagues, so you won't have to look far for ways to help students organize their writing; however, be cautious if using photocopies of organizers with empty boxes. This limits the students' thinking. If the organizer has four boxes but a student needs five, ideas may be left out. If it has four boxes and a student only plans to focus on three things, he may put in unnecessary information just to fill the box. Students usually use the number of lines on a page or the number of boxes given, no more and no less. This limits creativity, problem-solving, and writing.

Without practice, students who are asked to create their own organization charts instinctively will draw a circle or box first and then try to write in it. Instead, show students how to write down the idea, then draw a circle or box around the text. Showing them how to make the organizer fit a particular piece of writing, not have the writing fit within the given boxes, creates the tool they need for their writing and still allows them the freedom to make the piece their own.

Use the search term "graphic organizers for writing" online, and a plethora of organizers will be at your fingertips. Use those that work for you, but teach a variety to give students different experiences with organizing their thoughts on paper. Over time students' understanding of how graphic organizers work increases, and students will begin to make their own for each piece of writing. The goal is not to learn how to fill in a graphic organizer but, rather, to be able to *use* a graphic organizer to structure a piece of writing. As you teach different ways to organize writing for audiences, purposes, and genres, allow students to choose the organizers that make sense for them. Remember, photocopied or preprinted boxes and shapes are problematic for problem-solving and complexity of thought because they limit the possibilities.

Finally, be aware that students who struggle with writing can get stuck in the organization process. Bubbles and boxes become the task, and the story gets lost in the planning. Use individual conference time to help these students organize. Allow them to dictate their ideas orally, which can increase their speed and lessen their anxiety over the task. Writing takes practice; and when children struggle, practice is often not motivating. Scaffolding the process for those who need it is not about giving the student bubbles or boxes, but discussing and creating the structure together. With each subsequent piece, decrease the scaffolding until the student is organizing independently.

The examples below can be used to teach students to make the organizers work for their own writing (see figures 4.1–4.3). These are just a couple compared to those your district might have in mind, or that Google has to offer.

A graphic organizer should not be photocopied but, rather, drawn as you model how to use it in a mini-lesson. The number of boxes, categories, and details will depend on the individual piece of writing. Be sure to emphasize

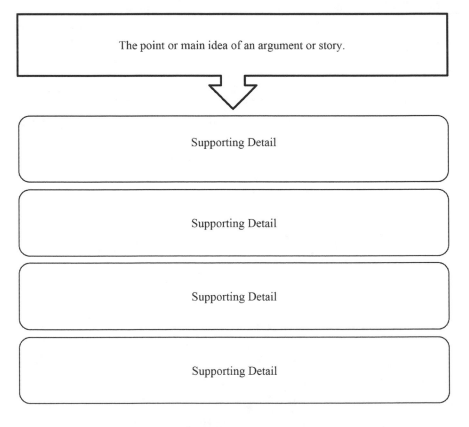

Figure 4.1.   A "What's the Point?" organizer will work for a story, informational piece, persuasive piece, or any type of writing that emphasizes a main idea, thesis, or point.

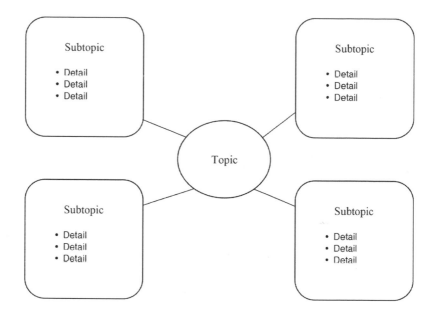

Figure 4.2. A "Topic Map with Categories" organizer works well with topics that are overarching, including several subtopics.

this point as you share each organizer, thinking out loud about your decision-making and goals for structuring the piece.

Remember, these organizers are not one-size-fits-all in writing. Each organizer is particular to the type of writing, and the number of boxes changes with each focus. The goal is to get students to organize their thoughts *before* they compose so that their pieces have a better structure than if they just did a freewrite. With freewrites, a student might have picked a topic, but without a structure in mind, he could end up with a mangled piece of random sentences. When students use organizers to help them compose the first draft, they only have to make sentences in the order or groupings the ideas are in already. Students can focus on composing sentences to get their pieces down and ready to revise.

What's the Point?

This type of organizer will work for a story, an informational piece, a persuasive piece, or any piece that emphasizes a main idea, thesis, or point. It is

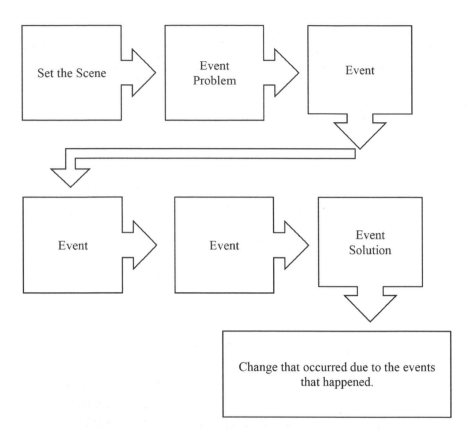

Figure 4.3. A "Story Flow Chart" organizer works well for a piece of fiction or a personal narrative, where events happen in sequential order.

important that the students understand that the number of supporting details will depend on the topic and the writer. Each piece will be different, so the number of boxes for supporting details will vary.

Topic Map with Categories

This organizer works well with topics that are overarching, including several subtopics. A piece about my dog would fit well with this organizer. My subtopics might be how the dog looks, what the dog eats, the tricks the dog does, and a funny event that involves my dog. A student also could use it for a piece on soccer. Subtopics might be the rules, the gear, the field, and scoring. The number of subtopics depends on the piece the student is writing.

Story Flow Chart

This organizer works well for a piece of fiction or a personal narrative, where the events happen in sequential order. Usually it involves a problem and a solution, or a lesson learned as well, and it is a good idea for the student to work it out before she starts to compose.

Cause and Effect Map

Cause and effect can be a difficult concept for students, especially when writing. The key with this kind of organizer is that the event (middle box) is the starting point. The students think backward to the causes of the event. Then they think forward to the effects of the event. This type of organizer is good for a science or social studies topic.

———⁓⁓⁓———

PLANNING JOURNAL: YOUR THOUGHTS ON ORGANIZING

Composing is so much easier when the details of the topic or story are organized beforehand. It may seem like organizing will add massive amounts of time to the writing process, but organizing will make drafting move smoother and be more coherent. Kathy likens organizing before drafting to combing her hair before she blow-dries it. If she doesn't comb it first, her hair will be dry but tangled. The same is true for writing. If students draft without organizing, they will have a draft, but chances are it will be a tangled mess that will take more work to straighten up. Plan how you will teach your students organizing.

- Which organizers will you teach for each genre?
- What is the right number of organizers for your particular class or grade?
- Look over your time line for the year and decide when you will teach organizing for each genre. Connect these with your plan for collecting lessons.
- How much choice will you give the students when using organizers?
- Who do you know will struggle to use the organization structures, and how will you remedy that?

- For your first mini-lesson on organizing, choose a topic you modeled in the first collection mini-lesson. Organize a text around that topic, thinking aloud about the decisions you are making. Plan this mini-lesson now, as this will be part of the mentor texts you will use when you teach about organization.

Chapter Five

Drafting

In first draft writing, students compose their ideas into a piece of writing. Drafting puts the heaviest mental load on students of all of the parts of writing workshop. Students have to form letters, spell words, compose sentences, space appropriately, insert punctuation, match the form of the verb with the subject, and put it all into one coherent piece. That's a lot to think about simultaneously, but our students do it—with varying results. Remembering where each student is in his writing progress and letting him know that your expectations are a bit more than he can do independently will help him gain autonomy when writing his first draft.

Getting the words and sentences down on paper is sometimes the hardest part. Many students think that the first draft must be perfect, a previous requirement. Professional writers always write a rough first draft, then change and rearrange it several times before the piece goes to the editor or publisher. Even then, the editor may send the piece back for changes.

Help students understand that the first draft needs to say what they want it to say about their chosen topic. Take off the pressure of perfection. Let students know that the paper does not have to be perfect, that punctuation and conventions will be taken care of with the third draft, that it's OK to spell words phonetically on the first draft. The first draft is where they put all of their ideas on paper. Help students focus on saying what they want to say on the first draft.

Using the organizer makes that job easier. When students first start writing workshop, especially if they are reluctant writers, have them make a sentence about each word or idea on their organizer. Have them write it in the

31

order they have designed on their organizer. When composing has a step-by-step procedure, students become more comfortable with writing a first draft. The blank paper isn't so scary, because they know what to write first, second, third, and so on. After the students have written a few pieces, they will become excited about writing the first draft because they are telling the world something that has meaning to them, and they know how to do it. They know the teacher will help them with anything they don't know how to do as they go through the process.

Writing is problem-solving. During the first-draft stage, students are solving the problem of writing what they want to say in the way that they want to say it. It's impossible to make a first draft perfect, so remind them not to try for perfection. Writing a first draft includes enough challenges without worrying about perfection.

When students are writing their first draft, remind them to not focus on spelling, punctuation, or capitalization. Assure them that you will help fix all of that later so that the paper will be their best work. Have them make their best word choices; they will have a chance to change words and sentences in the second draft. Have them spell the words the best they can; they will be able to fix the spelling in the third draft. Suggest that they compose as quickly as they can and still be able to read their own writing. Getting all of their ideas on paper is the goal.

Strategies designed to help students keep moving will help with the flow. Students can circle mistakes or uncertainties, reminding them that that word or sentence needs more work later. That lets you know a particular word or sentence or spelling was causing them trouble, so you don't have to guess the next thing to focus on in the conference. If the student struggles with something and marks it to let you know, then, that's the next thing to teach her. That makes your job easier.

The worry about spelling can be problematic for student and teacher. Students think about spelling the words they already know. But the words they don't know how to spell will be difficult and can stop them cold without permission to spell phonetically and move on. The teacher must have a strategy for when students ask, "How do you spell . . . ?" Have an idea how to handle the question, for once you spell the first word, there will be no end. It takes a while for students to quit asking for spellings, so stand your ground and make them handle it themselves in the first draft.

Students in early grades also are thinking about forming letters because handwriting is a fairly new skill they are acquiring. It is part of their process for this time in their development. So first and subsequent drafts take longer to write. Be patient. The more they write, the faster they will become. Be thankful that their stories are short, which also makes each stage move faster.

For questions about the length of the piece, tell students, "It needs to be as long as it needs to be to communicate your ideas." In other words, students need to make everything clear. Then they will be finished. At first students will be hesitant and uncertain. But once they have completed the entire process, students will understand that they determine the length and other parameters for their own writing, especially in the first draft. In conferences you can nudge students to lengthen or shorten their pieces for the sake of clarity, and students will see conferences as part of the process to make their pieces better.

These suggestions can make teachers uncomfortable. They want to help students succeed, and having them ignore errors seems to go against the teacher's role. But you and your students need to go through the process a few times before you become comfortable with postponing the corrections until the right time. No one produces a great piece of writing in the first draft. It is through the process that problems in the first draft are solved. The focus in first draft is getting all of the ideas on paper. Fixing and tweaking and changing will come later. First a writer needs to have something to fix and tweak and change before he can have an amazing piece of writing. That first draft is the foundation on which to build a great piece of writing.

Modeling drafting and composing in mini-lessons is an awesome way to show students the thinking that should take place while drafting. Write a draft in front of them, using a document camera or overhead, thinking aloud about your choices and how you use your organizer to help form the sentences and put connected sentences together into groups that will become paragraphs. You can model when you know the piece is finished, or how to handle uncertainties students struggle with as they compose their first drafts.

Struggling with your writing in front of students is important to their development as writers. Show them that even someone who is a competent writer struggles, thinks, makes mistakes, and works through issues. That gives them permission to struggle, think, make mistakes, and work through issues in their own writing.

Mini-lessons are great for addressing students' concerns. Showing students how to struggle through the first draft can help them realize that they aren't the only ones who struggle. You can have a mini-lesson on how to spell phonetically, letting them know that when they ask during the first draft you will say, "Spell it the best you can," or "Spell it the way it sounds." You will need to use this strategy *every* time. If you give in even once, other children will ask.

Using this strategy makes them think about how words are spelled, and they will pay more attention when they do find the correct spelling or see it in text because they have a purpose for using and spelling words correctly. Notice a mini-lesson is involved in whatever you see as an issue. In workshop methodology, lessons are short. It is simple to add ideas to mini-lessons as different needs arise in your classroom.

Writing a first draft is complex and time consuming. Encourage students as they work and struggle through the first draft. That is your role during this phase of writing workshop. In this part of writing workshop they are on their own, as only they can write their story.

—*ᴏᴠᴏ*—

PLANNING JOURNAL: YOUR THOUGHTS ON DRAFTING

Students do drafting. The teacher has little to do with this part of the process, except for mini-lessons and modeling to help them get started. The teacher's biggest job at this point is *not* to help during the writing. Teachers should not give students spellings or check each sentence. Instead, encourage them to keep writing, assuring them that it is OK to make mistakes at this point and that you will help them during the conferences. Use this journal entry to create an environment that allows for mistakes and misspellings during rough drafting.

- How will you set the stage for writing without worry while you encourage them to put their ideas on paper?
- What will be your standard answers and strategies when spelling questions arise?
- What standard answers and strategies will you use for how long the piece needs to be?
- Plan your first mini-lesson on drafting. Use the organizer you made in the mini-lesson on organizing. How will you show students the process of moving the ideas on the organizer to composing sentences, an important step for the students to learn but one that may not be apparent to novice

writers? Write the sentences of your first draft, planning how you will think aloud to show the students how to think as they compose. Ask and answer questions such as, How and where will you model misspelling words or making other mistakes?, then leaving them (or circling and marking with asterisks) as this is not the time to attend to those conventions? When the teacher moves forward in the face of mistakes, she helps students relax and be more comfortable with drafting and composing with their own mistakes.

Chapter Six

Revision Conferences

Students often struggle to understand the difference between editing and revising. Editing a piece is fixing grammatical, spelling, punctuation, and capitalization errors. Revising a piece means making changes that will make the meanings clearer and more understandable. Revising includes adding or deleting sentences, expanding sentences, changing words or wording differently, making connections, and showing by making pictures for the reader. It is here that students make their piece say exactly what they want to say.

Revising a piece of writing can be done many good ways, but not everything in any one piece needs revision. As the teacher, you need to figure out two things: First, what does the piece need most? Second, what will help the writer grow? Use these guiding questions to help you decide what to say to the student and lead him to the revision that will make each piece of writing better than the previous one, so he will show substantial growth from the beginning of the year to the end. When conducting a revision conference, it's good to focus on one big idea:

- Does the student's writing leave holes in understanding?
- Does is seem jerky?
- Does it get off to an unsteady start, leaving the reader wondering what the piece is about?
- Does it end flat, leaving the reader wondering why she read the piece in the first place?
- Does it need more detail?
- Does it need more emotion?

The questions will be many when you work with early writers, but focus on those that change the inner qualities of the piece. Focus there, not on the multitude of inevitable editing errors.

Once you have found a big-picture issue, focus on the few things the student can change to bring the big idea into focus. Revision conferences need to stay under five minutes. That way you can meet with more students during this time to keep everyone's work flowing. Don't revise too much during this conference; students respond better to a few things. A long list of things to revise may overwhelm them.

First, ask the student to read the piece aloud. This gives her a chance to review the piece like a writer and notice things she may not have realized while composing. Word choice and flow, for instance, are great for writers to hear for themselves.

As the student is reading, think about which way to steer the revision. Some teachers say, "Well, I like to let the student decide where to revise." Because the student is a novice in the process of becoming a better writer, you could throw away a chance for the student to learn something new about writing from the best writer in the room—you! Teaching is about moving students forward deliberately in their thinking and abilities. If they could do this by themselves, they wouldn't need teachers.

If a student cannot read her writing, then she will need to focus on rewriting for readability. If she is young or struggling, you might help her read it, filling in the missing parts as she helps you. You won't have to do this all year; students will improve throughout the year until they can read their writing to you. Use the rest of the time revising within the parts that were done, asking them to complete the rewrite.

REVISING WITH STUDENTS

After students have read, talk to them about things you noticed, didn't understand, or ideas that you might have for revision. As the teacher, you can suggest ideas for revision. As writers, students can choose exactly how they want to revise their pieces. Framing your suggestions as a choice ("You could do it this way or that way") or giving reasons why a revision would work well ("If you do it this way, it would make it clearer") puts the responsibility with the writer rather than the teacher.

Questioning the student about the story is another great way to get him to come up with the revisions in his own words, thereby retaining his voice in the piece. Question students about confusing parts, why they did a particular thing, the order of events, and other things only the writer can answer. Then ask the writer what he can do to clarify the meaning.

You or the student can write notes in the margins, draw arrows to move sentences or paragraphs, or mark any way that reminds the student what and how to revise once he has gone back to work. Avoid writing sentences on his paper; make the notes one word or a short phrase as a reminder of the discussion. The word will help the student remember the conversation, and he will compose the new sentence himself. Some teachers list on a Post-it note the things the student will do, and he keeps it when he returns to his desk. Then, when the child returns for the next conference, he takes the note with him and and it can be added to.

Some teachers object to writing on a student's paper, but professional writers do it all the time. Our memory of the English teacher bleeding red ink all over our writing might be why we dread the red pen, but the teacher was marking our papers to justify the grade. You are marking the paper to help the student improve.

As a writing teacher, you are helping the student through the process. So every mark you make on a draft (not on the published piece) is a reminder and a learning opportunity specific to students' thinking and writing. In the next draft, students will rectify their writing, making the new draft better than the first. This is change the students can see for themselves; that didn't happen on our papers of old. We were not given the rewriting opportunity after the teacher made comments; with workshop, we give students the chance to become better writers with our help, not our judgment.

Revision comes in many forms, and deciding what to help students focus on will be determined by the learner and the piece of writing. As every learner and every piece of writing is different, there are no scripts to follow. Your expertise as a teacher will guide you to decide the students' steps to revise a piece. At first learning the art of conferring is a bit hard. As you work through each conference, you will gain confidence and skill at helping students improve their writing. Trust yourself and the students to learn and grow. Know that there are patterns in the way that children grow as writers; use those patterns to help you lead the revising conference.

EXPANDING AND FOCUSING

With novice writers, consider one of two major ways to improve a piece of writing: expanding or focusing. Reluctant writers often write the smallest amount they can. In first or second grade, this may mean one sentence; in the upper grades, a few sentences. Accept this amount of writing and hold the revision conference to focus on expanding the piece.

Begin by asking questions about missing information. Jot down one word for each answer and circle it. Add as many details as you think the student can handle adding during the rewrite. Remember, they are reluctant writers: you want to push them forward but not give them too hard a task. The goal is to get them to finish with a piece that is better than the first draft, recognizing that even a small piece can be a better one.

Once reluctant writers begin to expand on their own, the problem of the order or sequence of events may pop up. The organizer can help with this problem, but the most reluctant writers still will have issues with order. These writers now remember to add more details, but the sentences are completely out of order. To draw arrows in an attempt to rearrange the sentences in a coherent order will only confuse the student further.

Sometimes it's best to cut the sentences apart and tape them back together in order, having the student help decide which sentence should go first, next, and so on. Students are puzzled at first, but after it's finished and they rewrite the second draft in this order, they chuckle about the state of their paper. This is the physical version of cut and paste, and it works really well dealing with a few sentences.

When rewriting, students will focus more on the order and better understand the structure of order in writing. You also may want to have a conference after these students organize. If they are having trouble with the order, clues to how to help might show up in the organizer. A discussion on how to order sentences from the organizer can help the first draft immensely.

During rewrites, it also might help to have students skip lines. This allows room to see the writing as well as to revise or edit clearly. Being able to circle parts or to write a note above the part to revise can help students rewrite.

With better writers, revision may be about finding a focus. Often they will write about a day that an event happened. Details about breakfast and dinner or a semi-connected trip to the grocery store are added as extra fluff. The story is there, in the middle of the fluff, stuck somewhere between the little happenings added like stamps to a passport. Help the students find that main story, delete extraneous information, and tweak the real story.

Sometimes a student will have more than one story. Once, Kathy had a student who wrote about three places she went during a vacation. The piece was eight pages long, and she had three stories! Such a piece is exciting for a teacher to see, but Kathy suggested the student write about one story this time. Her next piece could be about another of the places she visited, and she could even make the three pieces into a chapter book.

In the moment, the student wasn't too happy about cutting the other parts, but she was very pleased with her published piece after she had worked through the cuts and focused on her main story. Sometimes convincing comes through the work rather than through the teacher's solutions, but a teacher's suggestions were necessary to change the student's thinking so she could learn from that change.

LEADS AND ENDINGS

Once your students are writing focused pieces with good details, next look for a strong lead and/or a strong ending. Writers often have trouble with the beginning. Sometimes students will want to start the story with waking up and having breakfast, although breakfast has nothing to do with the story. All students will be different, and so asking them questions about their piece and their thinking are the best ways to help them find a beginning.

A good lead usually says something related to the topic that evokes the reader's interest and keeps him reading. A good way to get students to focus on a good lead is by asking the students who their readers are (usually the class and thus their peers) and something that might interest the readers and is related to the topic. Usually something general about the topic, an opinion most readers would agree with, can be a good place to start teaching them about good leads. If a student has written a piece about soccer, the lead sentence could be, "Millions of people around the world love soccer." The readers know the piece is about soccer. They also will think that if a lot of people love soccer, they might love it as well, so the piece might be good to read.

Students often begin a piece with a question. That can be an interesting lead, but usually it makes the writing sound as if the writer is not really interested in the topic. Moreover, a question lead is so overused by elementary students that it can cause the reader to lose interest at the start.

Get your students to try other kinds of leads. Using picture books or novels as mentor texts, notice what the author is doing with the first words or first paragraph. How is the author creating interest? Is the author painting a picture using imagery or drawing on a common emotion—maybe both?

As your writers improve, and you get better at conferring, you will be able to help them write more complex, more interesting leads. Writing good leads begins with knowing how others have started using good leads. Use mini-lessons to model using mentor texts that have varying types of leads. Using quality examples of text to showcase introductions hooks your writers into the process of writing good leads.

A good ending is a little trickier. Many students think that putting "THE END" as the paper stops means that the story ending is satisfying. A good writer wants the reader to finish the piece with a certain emotion or conviction. Something akin to a universal theme or a conclusion to a life lesson is the goal.

Nancie Atwell (2014) calls this "the Rule of So What?" It answers the question "Why should the reader care?" If a student has written a piece about her grandmother, a good ending will connect the reader through emotion. "My grandma will always be the wise woman that I will go to when life gets hard. She is the warmth and care when my world becomes unsteady." This ending juxtaposes warmth, care, and wise with hard and unsteady, bringing emotions to the surface and connecting back to the reader. Stories should have endings that answer why the piece was written.

Get students to state the point of the piece; it's a good place to begin a discussion about making a good ending. You might try some of these questions to lead a student to a good ending:

- What point are you trying to make?
- What do you want the reader to think or feel after reading your piece?
- How would you connect this to the world and make it a better place to live?

The last question isn't necessarily a literal question, but it will get students to think beyond their own life and move them out of the piece just enough to make a connection for the readers that will leave them thinking about the topic in ways they had not previously.

OTHER WAYS TO REVISE

At this point, thinking about revising conferences may be overwhelming, because it is not the same for each student. No specific rules apply to revising, which is why revising often gets skipped in the writing process. Editing is much easier; the rules are specific, the same for every piece of writing, so it is easier to focus more on editing. Every student is different in the way she thinks and is at a different point in her ability to write.

Think about one student in your class. What does he know about writing? What is the next thing he needs to know about writing? After he has learned that one thing, what next thing does he need to know? This is the best way to help students learn to revise—one step at a time. Asking yourself what the student knows and what he can do next helps you know what is next for each writer in your class. Each student is different, but learning about your students and teaching them are the two things you do all day every day. It is your profession, and you are an expert.

For all of these ways of revising, it is helpful if the students have skipped lines in their first draft and only written on one side of the page. Yes, they use more paper, but that way students can view and manipulate their work as a whole piece of writing that is in the process of becoming a good piece of writing. It is easier to write reminders or notes for revision between the lines and to cut apart sentences if the piece is out of order. It is also easier for the student to read during the conference. Skipping lines gives the teacher and the student space to revise.

These are just a few of many ways to revise a piece. No one way is the right way. Choose differently for each student and each piece. The guiding thought or vision: *think about what would make this student a better writer.* Revising conferences will become easier as you gain more experience. Don't try to be perfect or try to make the students' papers perfect; just work to move them forward in their thinking, learning, and writing. Revising conferences are the pinnacle of writing workshop. The conferences embody differentiation at its finest: each student gets the lesson at the time he needs it. Revising conferences focus on the writer, and the writers in our classrooms are the reason we teach.

———ɞɞɞ———

PLANNING JOURNAL: YOUR THOUGHTS ON
REVISION CONFERENCES

The revision conference is one of the most exciting parts of writing work-shop for the teacher as she attempts to create a writer of deep and complex ideas. The student needs to be led gently to improve the piece and his writing skills. Leading can be a little daunting at first, because no teacher's edition or script tells you exactly what to do with each student and each piece.

You must decide in real time what to teach. Pace yourself; in a first draft full of problems, every one need not be fixed. Trust yourself. Relax as you move through conferences; you know your students better than anyone, and your professional judgment will be on target. Once you find your rhythm and cadence in conferencing, revising with students is invigorating.

Use the first draft you wrote as a mentor text in your mini-lesson on drafting, and plan a mini-lesson on having a revision conference. This will give students an idea of how the revision conference will go, and they will see that even the teacher's piece needs revision. Many students are not used to writing several drafts or having conferences about their drafts, so students may have a hard time understanding the purpose of their first conference with you.

Use your draft to have a revision conference with yourself, using meta-cognitive talk about what might need to be changed to make the piece better. You may want to leave out important details, or put in extraneous informa-tion, during the modeling of drafting to give yourself talk in the conference about issues that students would have in their conferences.

Think about the students you have this year. Write their names and where you think they need to improve their writing (not conventions such as spelling, punctuation, capitalization, and grammar—that comes later). Look at the list below to help you think about the types of revision conferences you might have and what you might say in a revision conference. Does the student need:

- more details?
- to clarify the information?
- to take out extraneous information?
- to bring a focus to the piece?

- a better lead'?
- a stronger ending?
- transitions between paragraphs?
- a change in word choice?
- to rearrange sentences or paragraphs?

Chapter Seven

Revision Draft

After the revision conference, the student writes a second draft. Much of the first draft will be copied into the second draft, but the rest of the piece will be new, moved around, and improved. This is not just copying; it is revising. The conference serves as a teaching time and helps students focus on how to improve their pieces. You made suggestions, and students may have made decisions, but revising takes place as the students are writing the next draft. It is an active task.

The thinking, creativity, and problem-solving at this stage are phenomenal. Students are attending to the flow of the piece, making the piece better, and they know it. In the first draft students were thinking about how to compose sentences and say what was needed. In the revision draft, students take the writing and turn it into art. The conference points out inconsistencies, missing information, and weak parts. Rewriting allows the writer to make those weak parts clear and strong.

Students are thinking, working, and totally engaged. It is their writing—their art—and a doable task at hand. You may have suggested, but now students put new words and sentences on the page to make the changes that will bring their story to life. The results are almost magical as both teacher and students realize all that the students are able to do.

Require the full rewrite. It makes your students better writers. It also keeps them engaged long enough to allow the rest of the class to have conferences before the editing conference is needed. It is part of the process, and it should take some time. It is not just copying as the draft is becoming richer and deeper, and a new piece is emerging. Show the student (and yourself) the difference during the next conference by comparing the first and the second drafts side by side. Notice how the second draft is more complete and balanced. Rewriting allows students to gain understanding in the differences between revising and editing. You can tell them the differences repeatedly, but experiencing the differences brings better cognitive understanding. The rewrite is well worth the effort. They might balk at this at first, then, like any other habit, they know it comes next as they grow a better piece.

The exception to a full rewrite is a student having a second revision conference over only a small part of the piece. In this case, the student could just add the sentence or rearrange the words of that part, add to the ending or make whatever necessary small change. This would not be a major rewrite, just a tweak. All first revisions should entail bigger changes in making the piece say exactly what the students meant.

All students should have major revisions that require a complete rewrite—otherwise the learning is too small. A piece from a reluctant writer will have fewer revisions, but still require a full rewrite from that student because he works much slower. Students do not see how a piece is changed or better without rewriting the entire piece. Then the changes hit home, and the learning deepens.

A strong writer will have more to revise because the revisions will be more complex, and she can attend to more things at once. In this case, a full rewrite is necessary because the piece will have too many changes. If you look at a high-ability writer's piece and find little to revise because it is so much better than all of the other students' papers, reread it. View it as if a student from a higher grade had written it. What revisions does it need? If you aren't sure how to approach this, talk to a teacher one or two grade levels up and ask how she would revise the piece if the child were in her grade level. A different perspective on a high-ability writer's piece usually helps you find that sweet spot that pushes the student just enough to ensure growth.

Mini-lessons on how to revise and rewrite are extremely helpful to students. Work through a piece of your own that is marked for revision. Talk through the process as you rewrite; think aloud about your decisions and comment on finished sentences. Show students how to reread a revised sentence or paragraph to see the full effect of the revision. This rereading can reveal much about the flow, word choice, and meaning of a sentence.

Remember, don't focus on conventions such as spelling, punctuation, capitalization, or grammar yet, so students can view someone intentionally choosing not to focus on them at this time. You may acknowledge a misspelled word by circling it or putting an asterisk next to it, but then refocus on the task at hand: revising. As you share your writing in the mini-lesson, and talk about how to make it deeper and more complex, make sure you only do a small part—five minutes maximum. This will show students that they can always do more; good revision takes time, and from it better writing emerges.

Revisions are part of the hard work of writing; rewards are the major improvements in the students' writing. Students are doing this hard work, so they need time to revise and rewrite. After a few pieces, the students will see the value of revising and rewriting. They will see how the process works and become totally engaged in it. Giving students this time to revise is integral to growing good writers.

———❦———

PERSONAL JOURNAL: YOUR THOUGHTS ON REVISION DRAFT

Revising is creative problem-solving, and students must be the ones doing the work. Once students have conferred with you about possible revisions, they need time and space to revise their pieces. Think about how you can set up this time and space for the students. At first some students will not like having to rewrite, but it is important that you find ways to encourage them through rewrites of the first crucial pieces. As students write more and revise more, they begin to see the value in revision. Then rewriting becomes a more natural part of their process.

- Why are complete revisions and rewrites necessary for this draft?
- Write down ways you can support or encourage students as they work through revision.
- Look at your mentor text and rewrite it, making the revisions that you noted during your own revision conference. This is the best way to put yourself in your students' shoes. Notice the details of what you are thinking as you rewrite and revise, so you can target and help the students during this important phase. Make notes about the metacognitive talk you will have during the mini-lesson that models rewriting and revising.

Chapter Eight

Editing Conference

7

Finally, we get to the work on the conventions of writing: grammar, punctuation, capitalization, and spelling. Editing is late in the process for a reason. During drafting, if students attend to conventions it will hinder the thought process of putting the ideas on paper. As adults, we developed automaticity for periods, spellings, and other conventions (at least the common ones) because we have had so much practice with conventions. Thus, we can correctly use basic punctuation as we write with little thought.

Elementary grade students have not had much experience with conventions, neither in reading nor in writing. (Kindergarten students have had no experience with these conventions.) Older students may have had bad experiences with conventions—maybe their papers were marked all over in red or purple because they used incorrect conventions, or worse, they received a lower grade because they misspelled a word. When students have experiences that inhibit their word choice, such as spelling incorrectly or not knowing how to spell a word, they will quit trying to use a variety of words in their writing. Giving them permission on the first and second drafts to not think about the conventions frees them to think about what they are saying and how they are saying it.

It is very important in a student's understanding of the process of writing to separate revising and editing into two very distinct processes. Drafting and revising focus on what is said and how it is said; editing for conventions makes it easier for readers to understand what is being said. Revising is varied and different and can be done in as many different ways as there are students and pieces of writing. Editing consists of rules to be followed the same way every time the rule is used. Confusing the two will only hinder students as they learn to write.

Students want to write correctly, but having them attend to everything in their pieces at once is confusing and overwhelming. Tell them not to worry about conventions in the first two drafts. Assure them that you will help them with conventions later. That allows students to focus on the communication first. Later, when they focus on conventions, they will be directly associated with their own writing, transferring the rules effectively into their writing and into their brains for future use. Because students see conferring happening daily, they feel safe that you will help make their draft good before it is published or shared. This is one way to build trust in your classroom as part of school life.

Editing makes the piece easier for the reader. Readers use grammar, punctuation, capitalization, and correct spellings to help them decode and thus comprehend what is written. If a piece has poor grammar, punctuation, capitalization, and misspelled words, the reader may become frustrated with trying to grasp the meaning and give up. Because conventions have rules that are followed the same way each time, these conferences are very straightforward; students are told what to put in or take out and why.

The goal of the conference is to help students with the conventions needed in the specific piece of writing. In revision, you ask questions; then students talk about what they want to convey. Notes are made, and students decide what to change in their writing. Editing involves no decisions; it is done correctly and makes the paper easier to read.

Students will learn those rules for conventions in three ways:

The first way has to do with reading for fluency. When students read good literature, they are exposed to good uses of capitalization, punctuation, grammar, and correctly spelled words. Students who rarely read are rarely exposed to these conventions, so they do not gain a more intrinsic knowledge of how conventions work. Having students read more and helping them with their fluency and prosody will help them become better and more automatic at using the conventions in their own writing.

Mini-lessons on capitalization, punctuation, and grammar can be covered based on the needs of the whole class and often align with the scope and sequence of your school or grade level. Once taught, certain expectations need to surround the use of the conventions. Depending on the grade level, skill level, and experience of the writer, you can expect students only to try them, or to do them correctly.

This is another point of differentiation based on the needs and goals of each student. After the teacher presents the concept, it does not necessarily mean the concept is learned. Students first need to have experience with it. If you had taught it several times and had several conferences addressing a particular rule with students, then expect students to use it in their writing without prompting; however, if you've only taught it once and the conference is over that convention, then gentle reminders are in order.

Editing conferences should be viewed as reminders. As you confer with students about edits, explain why they should use a certain convention. Using editing marks to help students correct their errors, rather than marking the errors for a grade, gives the students a chance to correctly use the conventions before grading.

Before any editing conferences, share your editing marks with the students. Students can make a chart and fill it in during a mini-lesson. Then it can be put into the notebook as a resource (figure 8.1). Students will use this resource until they have a solid foundation of the rules for the conventions of writing.

This chart can be presented through a mini-lesson, but other mini-lessons you present will help with different conventions. The best way is to show students that mentor texts use examples from good pieces of literature, as looking at the conventions used correctly by published authors gives the correct way to use capitalization, punctuation, and grammar. Talk through the mentor text, telling students what the author did and why.

In an editing conference, you can read the piece aloud sentence by sentence. Each time you come to a mistake, talk specifically about that convention and its need in that place. Then put the editing mark on the paper. Do this throughout the entire paper, telling the rule and using the editing mark on the error to remind the student what he needs to fix. This talk is specific to his writing, so it is more meaningful. It also helps the student better understand the convention as well as the need to use it. Because the rules for conventions are consistent, and conventions always are needed to aid the reader's comprehension, it makes sense for the writer to use them, but scaffolding is a necessary process as it is not something that comes naturally.

Many teachers are shocked that we would suggest "bleeding ink" all over the paper, remembering that English teacher who "bled" all over our paper along with the giant circled C at the top. The red marks were to prove the

Editing Marks	
 ⚡	delete/ take off
 ∧	insert
 ¶	new paragraph
 ⊙	insert a period
 ⋀	insert a comma
 ≡	make a capital letter
 ⋀	insert a space
 ⌣	put together
 ⓈⓅ	correct spelling
 ∿	switch the order
 ∨	insert an apostrophe

Figure 8.1.   Editing marks chart.

grade. And because the grade was final, there was no point in showing us all of our mistakes lacking the opportunity to correct them.

Editing in writing workshop is not about mistakes; it's about learning to make writing easy to read for the reader and helping writers find their mistakes on their own as they grow. Editing, therefore, is done before grading, and corrections are made before grading. At conference the teacher can remind the student of conventions they are learning.

Editing and "bleeding" differ in two ways. When editing, the teacher explains the convention and marks a reminder on the page; the student corrects the conventions before the paper is graded, allowing for learning to take place. It is from the teaching by a knowledgeable other—you, the best writer in the class—that learning happens. No matter the color pen; it matters that students can see the mistakes, make changes, and grow as a result. Writing workshop is a growth-oriented model.

An incorrect assumption is that the teacher is giving students the answers if she edits, and students only have to copy the answer. This is not it exactly. The teacher makes the editing mark. Students either have to know the mark or look it up, then transfer the correct form onto their next draft. This is heavy scaffolding on the teacher's part, but it leads students to internalize the concepts. Students slowly begin to incorporate the concepts into their writing with each subsequent piece. Fewer and fewer mistakes appear as students produce more and more pieces.

After a few conferences in which a convention was explained and corrected in the next draft, require students to incorporate the correct convention on subsequent pieces. Put the onus on them; this will help students become more responsible. Your expectations will help them become more conscious of how they use conventions and thus become better writers as they think of the rules that help readers enjoy their writing.

Most students will work at a convention on their own and begin to use it correctly after just one conference, because their expectations sometimes are greater than ours. Students want to use conventions correctly as it is important that their writing be good. Simple lessons correcting mistakes in sentences don't help students transfer the knowledge of these rules into their own writing, but connecting these lessons to the students' writing does help.

The big question: How much should you edit student writing? Teachers don't want to overwhelm students with too much to edit, nor do they want students to publish with too many mistakes. The answer depends on who your students are and their abilities at the time of editing. This will be a professional decision only you as the teacher can make. With each piece, you will learn more and more about the student as a learner and a writer. No one-size-fits-all method helps in deciding what to edit and what to leave for another time; the more you understand each student, the better your conferences will be.

Early on we both decided to edit all of the mistakes on all the of students' drafts. Kathy's reasoning was that she didn't want bad habits to form from lack of correction. Jenny's reasoning was that she wanted the children to be able to read their own writing easily as well as trust that their piece would be readable when sharing time came.

Today we still edit everything, but we have pedagogical reasons for it. Weaver, Bush, Anderson, and Bills (2006) state that editing conventions in conferences have long-term effects on students' abilities with conventions. Experience also has shown that this process does scaffold the concepts and that most students do internalize the rules and begin using them on their own, so each subsequent editing conference brings fewer convention errors than the previous one. This means that students have internalized the rule; not only are they using it in their writing for writing workshop, but for writing in other subjects as well. This internalization of the rules is deeper learning that is transferred to other areas.

One more reason for editing everything is that when a reluctant writer, reluctant worker, or a new English learner publishes a piece she has corrected completely, she is proud of her work. Some even have commented, "My story looks just as good as the [smartest student's] piece does." That kind of pride does not come easily to these students, so when it happens it's a defining moment in a teaching career.

As you gain more experience with editing conferences, you will see patterns in the mistakes students make. Sometimes many mistakes seem to remain after editing; but on closer inspection, students make the same mistake repeatedly. The most common recurring error is not using periods. This is especially true of young writers. Marking each mistake and then talking to the student about how it is happening again and again can be powerful in getting him to pay closer attention to that particular convention in the next piece.

Sometimes you notice conventions are correct in some places and incorrect in others in the same piece of writing. This means the student is not paying close attention to conventions and is sloppy when writing this draft. Bringing attention to this inconsistent use of conventions is a good way to help students internalize the use of conventions at all times, and learning to pay attention to the conventions at this point moves the student toward automatically applying convention rules as we do as adults.

As students become more comfortable with the writing process, you begin to notice more complex mistakes. This means that the student is taking risks and trying out new ideas. Students who are taking risks with commas and semicolons are thinking about ways to make their writing more complex. This movement toward more complex sentence structures is almost unheard of when teaching through prompts or more traditional ways of teaching writing, but it almost always happens with stronger or older writers. This is powerful learning because the student is extending her own knowing. This is exactly what students should be doing as they refine their craft.

Conventions make writing easy for the reader and listener to understand. If students are writing authentic pieces for an audience beyond the teacher, then they need to use conventions correctly. Students intrinsically understand this when they have authentic audiences, as they truly want the audience to read and enjoy their pieces. Writers above all else want to be understood, and conventions help make that happen.

SPELLING

Spelling is a unique convention of writing. It is ingrained in the history of education and has been its own subject since the inception of public school. The focus of spelling instruction over the years has been to memorize the spelling of words. The instruction over the years has been to teach spelling outside of writing, as its very own entity.

For more than a century our schools have taught spelling by giving a weekly list of words to study, assignments that supposedly help students with spelling words such as writing each word five times, and then testing at the end of the week. The tests are graded, and the following week the students receive a new list to memorize for the week. Although this practice does not increase a person's ability to spell words correctly when he writes, it has continued as the primary way to teach spelling.

Spelling has a purpose, and that purpose is to make writing readable and understandable. If the goal of spelling is to make reading increasingly understandable and convey particularities to its readers, then it needs to be integrated into the writing process so that students can use their spelling knowledge in the context where it matters. We need to think deeply about where and when to focus on spelling. As students are writing their first drafts, they know when they do not know how to spell a word. This is a good skill to have when learning how to spell better, but focusing on spelling in the first draft hinders the flow of the writing. Instead, help students develop a mind-set of "not now, but later," to put the emphasis in the right place. Having students correct spelling during editing will bring utility to an area that has been separated from writing for way too long.

The easiest way for students to spell something is to ask the teacher. As teachers, we often spoon-feed information to students. Although sometimes difficult, learn to say, "Spell it the best you can" and "We will correct it later." At first it is hard to convince students you will help them with the spelling later in the editing conference, but after they have gone through the process a couple of times, they will quit asking. Students need to experience the process and have teachers help them spell words at the appropriate time to be able to trust the process and the teacher. Be mindful of this; once one child has heard you answer how to spell a word, many other voices soon will follow!

Mini-lessons on strategies for finding the correct spelling of a word can really help. Present mini-lessons on sounding out words by modeling through some writing and pretending to struggle over words. This will go a long way toward making them independent spellers through the second and third drafts. When they do ask for the spelling of a word, you can then remind them about the strategy of sounding out the word and spelling it based on the sounds they hear when they say the word.

Present mini-lessons on using resources such as word walls to show students how they can find the correct spelling many times without asking the teacher. Again, model composing and coming upon a word that you cannot spell; looking around the room, or remembering that you had seen the word in a book; going to that book to find that word and, thus, the correct spelling of the word. When students are confronted with this problem, they will remember your actions and follow your example.

Presenting spelling lessons where you group words with the same spelling pattern and focus on that pattern will help students gain competence in using those patterns to help them spell words. In addition to the mini-lesson, make an anchor chart with those specific words and the pattern used to spell them. Hang this on the wall, reminding students that it is a resource to use when they don't know how to spell a word. When they ask you about a spelling, you can redirect them to the resource on the wall.

Their best resource is in knowing that you will help them during the editing conference. This trust helps them become risk-takers with their vocabulary and, eventually, better spellers. But even in the editing conference, you can ask them what resources they can use, pushing them to be more independent spellers. Phonetic spellings, spelling patterns, and using resources can help students on this journey for independence.

Strong readers often are good spellers because they see words often, but they also notice patterns in spellings and use these patterns to figure out new words. Your good readers probably also are your good writers. They won't need much help in spelling. You probably can give them the spelling, point out a pattern, and they will internalize it quickly. These are the writers you will want to challenge with more specified vocabulary and deeper, more complex word choice. Encourage them to use more complex vocabulary in their writing and spur them on with positive feedback.

Your reluctant writers, on the other hand, will make many spelling errors. For these writers, use a variety of techniques—don't just spoon-feed them the words. Give them most of the misspelled words during your conference just to make the process run smoother and faster, as reluctant writers usually are slower writers and finishing pieces is a great motivator for keeping them writing. Then pick out one or two words for which they must use one or more strategies to find the right spelling. Ask questions about where students might find such a word (word wall, science notebook, reading group, etc.) and lead them to the strategy that will work to find the spelling for that word.

If you have taught lessons on using the dictionary, then you might choose one word for them to look up. Using the dictionary takes the longest amount of time, so use it for only one word to make the task manageable. Also make sure it is a word in which the first three or four letters are phonemically correct; otherwise students may never find it in the dictionary. Teaching students to use resources to find correct spelling—and when to use those resources—will make the process of writing smoother and help students become better spellers.

A note about spelling: it is often taught decontextualized, meaning using spelling books. These spelling books pattern words but do not provide context. As teachers, we try to engage children in creating context by having them write the word in a sentence or even a paragraph. Then we are upset when the children score 100 percent on their weekly spelling test but use the very same words incorrectly in their writing. This happens for two reasons.

First, students need to learn word meanings in context. Reading and writing gives them the context, and it is within a topic in which they are engaged. Second, spelling is about learning how words work. In order to do that, students need plenty of practice in reading that involves manipulation, segmentation, chunking and myriad other phonological skills for it to be transferred to another space, such as writing.

You can follow up on those skills in workshop, even teach them in short bouts, but it is in working with words that children learn how patterning and derivation of words affect spelling. Spelling, adjusted, followed-up on, and helped through workshop will happen over time with words students use often, but words must be taught and used in context. Writing workshop is one place for that accountability.

—◦◦◦—

PLANNING JOURNAL: YOUR THOUGHTS ON EDITING CONFERENCE

The conventions of standard English are the same every time and everywhere. Conventions help readers understand the message in the writing. Knowing the rules for conventions is a goal for students so they can focus on conventions at the right times, reducing anxiety when writing, and allowing writing to be more enjoyable. When we are stressed about it "looking right," or "getting it right the first time," our writing is stilted; many students become overwhelmed and lose motivation. Write a plan for moving your students toward a better understanding of how the rules of written language work while holding true to the fact that conventions are helpful but not the only way a teacher must engage with the work.

- First write about how you feel making editing marks to correct the convention mistakes on students' papers. If it makes you uncomfortable, do you think experience might make it easier or change the way you feel? If you have reservations (which you need not), what is your plan to let students know what the corrections will be and hold them accountable for the conference and their work?
- During the revision conference section of this text, you listed each student and an area for him to work on. Use that same list/chart to add a penciled

number to indicate how many minutes you imagine the editing conference should take with each student. This can act as a guidepost for differentiating between students' needs.

- How will you use word walls, dictionaries, and other resources to help with spelling?
- What mini-lessons on conventions will you have during the year—early, in the middle, and in the latter part of the year?
- Use your mentor text to plan the first lesson on how an editing conference will happen. Make sure your piece has common and uncommon mistakes for all of the conventions of writing. Think about your metacognitive talk as you mark all of the mistakes and explain why the grammar, punctuation, capitalization, or spelling needs to be changed. If students see that you marked up your paper to fix the errors, they will be ready for errors on their papers to be marked for fixing.

Chapter Nine

Edited Draft

Now that students have a paper with editing marks inserted in various places, the goal is to rewrite the piece exactly as it is, making the corrections where the editing marks are. This is the third time the students will rewrite their papers. Although it may seem a little tedious—especially the first couple of times writers are asked to engage in this rewriting behavior—the power is in having the students polish their pieces to near perfection.

By this point, the words have been written and tweaked and changed. The ideas are flowing smoothly and are clear in their intent. Before this point, the writing mostly was about the writers expressing themselves and communicating ideas. With editing, the focus now is clearly on the reader or listener. The best expression of ideas cannot be shared if writers do not adhere to the conventions of the language. If periods are left out, sentences become ambiguous. If words are not spelled correctly, the reader will stop and struggle to understand. If commas are misplaced or missing, the meaning could change drastically. Students need time to work through thinking this way about conventions. In addition, when the writer of the piece becomes the reader, he too will struggle if it has not been polished.

Don't rush this part of the process. Allow a child to erase mistakes and correct them. Making the student rewrite the piece with corrections is integral to helping him understand how the conventions work. It will take more time to rewrite, but the writing for this piece and the next piece will be better. Students need time to think about conventions to understand the rules. Because we are in such a hurry to cover the curriculum and prepare the students for "the test," we often forget to give them time to think about what they are doing. Students need to make meaning from the tasks we give them and the new concepts they are learning, which only occurs with time spent using and struggling with new concepts to incorporate new learning into the old ways of doing things.

Model this rewrite with your own piece of writing to help the students understand how to think about conventions. Thinking aloud as you rewrite and correct spelling, punctuation, capitalization, and other conventions shows students what to expect during this phase of the writing process and emphasizes thinking through the grammatical process of writing as a meta-cognitive task that, in the end, rewards both writer and reader.

Model using your editing chart. Show students how to use the chart to figure out what to do with the editing mark. Stop at the mark, check the chart, match the rule for when and why the rule needs to be adhered to, and then incorporate the correct convention into the sentence as it is rewritten. Showing those steps will help students understand what to do and why it is important. It gives students a step-by-step process to engage in when rewriting their own pieces and the power to do it.

You can use a mini-lesson to model how to use a word wall as a resource. The words on your word wall—appropriate to grade level and class needs—should be ones students might need help to spell correctly. At kindergarten and first-grade level, the words mostly will be high frequency words such as "the," "a," and "of," as those are the words students are learning to read as well as write. At higher grade levels, the word walls can use similar spelling patterns that students are learning, or vocabulary from reading, science, and social studies lessons.

However you structure the word wall, it should be easy to read from anywhere in the room and easy to find the specific word the student is seeking. Size of the letters, spacing between words, and chunking of similar words all make a difference in the ease or difficulty of using the word wall as a resource. Consider using small word walls that can be put up when students are learning the words and taken down when students have mastered the words and are in need of new ones.

If you want students to use a dictionary, model in a mini-lesson or two how to find a word in the dictionary. If students are given a long list of words to look up in the dictionary, this can be a tedious task. But when students use the dictionary to check the spelling or meaning of a word they want to use in their own writing, the task can be not only useful but enlightening. When they need one word, they will focus on the search; they also will find that the dictionary holds far more new and interesting information about the word. When modeling, show students the different pieces of information, such as the word derivation, synonyms and antonyms, syllabication, and so on.

Using books or other reading materials to find words is a little more specific and difficult, depending on the student, the word, and the reading material. It only will occur if the student needs a word and remembers that she read it recently, and where. You still can model this as you edit a piece in front of the students. As you rewrite, stop at a misspelled word and think aloud through the process; or remembering, then searching for the place where you recently saw the word in a book or other text. This strategy can be powerful as students learn that words can be transferred from anywhere.

Once students have finished writing this draft, have them read the pieces to themselves, either aloud or silently. Encourage them to notice how their piece flows smoothly, much better than their first draft. Students now become the readers and can truly understand how conventions make the reading easier. Students also can see the fruits of their labor and understand why they went through the process, the conferences, and the rewrites. You want them to acknowledge this reward, especially in the beginning. It will help to instantiate that their work rewriting and conferring was worth it.

The thinking that happens during this polishing time will make students better at all of the conventions. As they rewrite and correct, they will think about a particular convention—how it is used, where it is used, and why it is used. No need to tell them to think about it; they will do it on their own as part of the rewriting process. Over time, the corrections become internalized as they are in the context of the students' own writing. The conventions become real, and students use them more and more frequently with each subsequent piece of writing until they are automatic. That is the goal of every writing teacher, and it happens through the practice of scaffolding by the teacher in real writing, not prewritten sentences from a language book or worksheet.

At this point, you may decide to end the process, and this draft is the published piece. The piece is complete and can be read and enjoyed by peers. However, you can have students make books for the publishing part of the process. Young students, of course, love making picture books out of their writing, but even fifth graders enjoy the creative process of making books. It adds a final writer's touch to the writing process. The goal is to publish every piece, but not every piece needs to be made into a book.

—◦◦◦—

PLANNING JOURNAL: YOUR THOUGHTS ON THE EDITED DRAFT

Students need time to fix their convention mistakes so that the rules of conventions become ingrained in their writing. It is the most direct part in the entire process. Students are following a set of rules and doing exactly what is needed to make the piece readable based on your editing marks.

- At this point the expectation should be that all edits are corrected because you have taken into account the abilities of the students. How will you grade the conventions? Will you explicitly state which conventions will be graded? (More on this in chapter 19.)
- Look at the mentor text you created. Rewrite it now, thinking about how you will model rewriting and what your metacognitive talk will be as you make corrections.
- How will you decide which draft will just be published and which will go on to become a book? Will there be times when you do and times when you don't allow making books?

Chapter Ten

Publishing Conference

If you or the students decide to take the process one step further, then putting the text into a student-made book will give students an opportunity to learn about design, illustrations, and the structure of picture books. Publishing in book form is the part that students love the most. Students are making a book that in their eyes is every bit as awesome as a published picture book. It has a cover and a title page. It has illustrations. And because they have gone through the writing process, it tells a really good story. This part says, "I have arrived as a writer!"

When students look at the finished piece, polished and published, they will be amazed at their ability to write, and you will feel that it is an accomplishment. This is why it is so important to go through the writing process for every single piece. It is an important accomplishment for the teacher as well!

Making books can add a day or two to the process, so you decide when a book should be published. Publishing once a month or every six weeks will give publishing a special emphasis. Let students choose which piece to publish. Because you are cutting out a portion of the process, the students will produce more pieces and thus have more experience composing, revising, and editing. Having the students publish every piece, however, adds another layer of thinking to the process. The students will be thinking about design, paragraphing, and illustrating, and will begin looking at picture books in a more in-depth way, considering layout and other aspects.

If students write a poem, a letter, a critique, or a blog post, then a book would not work. A poem can have a frame and an illustration or be put into an anthology. A letter needs to be mailed or e-mailed to create a purpose for writing it. A critique can be put near the book shelf, or a class wiki created for students to access when they are looking for a good book to read. If students are interested in being an expert on a topic, they can start a blog post centered on the chosen subject. Publishing needs to match the genre and give the writer an opportunity to be read, whether the author reads it aloud to an audience or finds individual readers.

Because every piece needs a reader, publishing needs to take the reader into account. A reader needs a piece that has easy-to-read handwriting or font, correct conventions—and, most important, a story or a flow that is of interest. At the elementary level, illustrations are important, and even fifth graders love to read stories with illustrations.

Saving publishing for a time when everyone chooses one piece of writing and makes a book simultaneously breaks up the flow of the writing process. It brings new problems, such as stopping and starting a piece after several days or weeks. It also creates a facilitation problem for you, as many students may need help at the same time rather than the staggered timing that provides a pattern and rhythm that keeps things moving. If you do not want students to make a book for every piece, you can stipulate one piece in a genre, or that every third piece can be made into a book. This allows only a couple of students to make a book at the same time. Supplies are easier to manage, as are the children. Others in the class are motivated by seeing their friends make books and will want to make it to that stage as well. This will help to keep the flow of writing workshop going at a steady pace.

Making a book involves much learning, such as design, connecting pictures to text, and paragraphing. Making books connects reading to writing in ways that nothing else can. The concepts that students learn in reading lessons directly connect to the concepts they learn in writing workshop. Many "aha!" moments come as students make books from their writing. The process need not be elaborate; in fact, make it as simple as possible so as not to create more work for yourself. In the students' eyes, stapling blank copy paper to construction paper for the front and back covers makes awesome books. Students can decide in the publishing conference on the color, size, and even shape of their books. Staple the pages right then and there (see figures 10.1 and 10.2). Don't spend hours ahead of time making blank books, as each student's book will be a different number of pages. In the conference, decide on how many pages, pull the exact number, and staple them inside the covers. That only takes about a minute and is more convenient than making a bunch of generic books at one time.

Students can easily publish every piece as it will add only a day or two to their entire writing process. Publishing every piece is exciting for the students, and it is a great motivator to get them to focus and move faster through the process. Publishing each piece also keeps a better flow, as it is always part of the process. When it is the next step, students move easily into publishing with the goal of sharing with the class. A lot of literacy thinking is involved in publishing, so it is a viable means to an end.

For more experienced children, publishing using technology might be an option. Currently, most students have facility with a keyboard and often use a computer or tablet at home. As teachers, facilitating writing in real ways and for real readers means that we must allow for, even promote the use of the computer for publishing. If a teacher wants to ensure that the responsibility for publishing the book through typing is on the student, the student must know how to do three things.

First, students must know how to open and create a document in a word processing program. Second, they must know how to use spell check correctly (even though they have worked through spelling on their own, invariably they will make mistakes while typing). And, finally, they must know how and where to save their documents. The responsibility for this last step cannot be overstated. Many have lost documents by leaving them open waiting for a teacher to save them, deleting them accidentally, or forgetting to save them altogether. The onus must be on the student. Small reminder sheets will help after you have had mini-lessons in the computer lab. Ask if you have a lab teacher to help students practice these skills. Or when in the lab yourself, practice these skills before moving on to another lesson that might be required while you are there. Teachers must help facilitate technology use in real ways, and publishing books is one of those ways.

MENTOR TEXTS AND MINI-LESSONS

The focus of a publishing conference is to design a book. Therefore, looking at the paratext and illustrations of authentic children's literature are essential in helping students make good design decisions. The paratext is everything that is not part of the story. The cover, the title page, the end pages, and the dedication are all part of the paratext. All of these things help a reader decide to read a book, and they can be addressed through mini-lessons. The illustrations help tell the story, and often they are such an integral part of the story that it could not be told completely without them. Show students how interaction between text and illustrations make the story richer; that relationship sets the tone and standard for publishing.

Using picture books as mentor texts to point out these traits and to look at how the book is designed gives your students a more complex look at the processes and decisions that go into making a published book. This will make the process of making decisions about design in their own books a deeper endeavor, producing an overall effect that is much more complex and rooted in what good readers and writers do. Knowing that different authors, illustrators, and publishers design books differently can also give students the freedom to try new techniques and come up with various ways of publishing their own pieces.

Having mini-lessons on book design will give students tools they need to think deeply about their own craft and that of others. Be sure to include a mini-lesson on how you would turn your own writing into a book. Thinking out loud about your thinking and decisions can give students their own inner talk as they move through the process. This inner voice naturally will become part of the students' process not only in publishing, but also in other parts of the process. Eventually students will begin to work on pieces with the end in mind, thus creating complexity and more meaningful pieces of writing. In your mini-lessons, consider the following questions:

- What is on the cover? Why did the illustrator choose that picture or design?
- What is on the title page?
- What font and size did the illustrator choose?
- Are the end pages blank, or do they have pictures?
- Where are the pictures on each page?
- Where is the text on each page?
- Do the pictures help tell the story? Do they tell more than the text?
- How do the pictures go with the text? Do I need pictures to enhance my text?
- Do the pictures and the text tell a complete story?

These questions help you focus your mini-lesson on one or two related aspects of publishing and make your teaching clearer. The more precise your mini-lesson, the more likely students will remember the concepts you taught.

DURING THE PUBLISHING CONFERENCE

Making books is the next step after the editing rewrite, so the publishing conference is the first step in publishing. By this time, you will be completely familiar with the student's piece. You won't need to read it through when the child comes to conference. Begin by asking what kind of book the student would like to make. Small? Large? A big book? A shaped book?

Next, ask what color the student would like for the cover. Books can be different sizes. Two 9-by-12 pieces of construction paper can be used for the front and back covers, with plain paper stapled in between. One piece of construction paper and the plain paper can be folded in half to make a smaller book. The paper can be folded in half, cut and then folded in half again to make a tiny book (figure 10.1). If you have access to larger construction paper, students can choose to make big books, using large white construction paper for the inside pages. This is the easiest way to put together books, and you only need small supplies of copy paper and construction paper.

Shape books can be made with a little more work on your part (figure 10.1). The shape should match the content of the piece. Books about baseball, snakes, whales, puppies, and kittens make good shape books. You can draw a simple shape onto a manila folder and cut it out to make a pattern for the students to trace (figure 10.2). Put together a construction paper book as you would with a basic book. Then have the student use the pattern to trace the shape and then cut it out through all of the layers. This will help the book have even edges, and it takes less time for the students to cut it out. Shape books should not be much smaller than a regular sheet of paper as the students need room to write and illustrate, and the shape sometimes takes away that space.

Take the edited draft and determine how many pages the book will need to be. Circle and number the groups of sentences that will go together on a page. Usually these are paragraphs if the students are older, or what could be a paragraph for younger students. For very young students, only one or two sentences might be on each page. Now you know how many pages the book needs.

Students can write and illustrate on the front and back of each page, but you and the student need to make that decision, depending on the illustration materials. If markers are allowed in publishing, they bleed through the paper, making the reverse side useless. For this reason, you may want to restrict the use of markers. Count out the right number of plain white pages for the book

Figure 10.1.   Sample books.

and staple them together with the cover pages. If it is a shape book, the student will trace the pattern and cut out all of the pages together so that it looks like a finished, special piece.

Go through the book and point out the parts students need to work on, such as the cover and title page. Then number the pages in the book corresponding to the edited draft. Young children need reminders each time for which text goes on each page. They also need reminders that they need to copy the text exactly from their edited draft and use their best handwriting so that readers can enjoy the book. After several published pieces, older students may be able to make decisions on which text goes on each page and how many pages they need before they come for a conference.

Also talk about the placement of the illustrations. Will the illustrations be at the top of the page and the text at the bottom, or vice versa? Will this be the same on every page, or will it vary from page to page? Remind students to write the text first and illustrate second. This will ensure enough room for

Figure 10.2. Book patterns made from file folders.

neatly printed text; when students draw the illustrations first, sometimes they don't leave enough room for the text that was planned for that page.

Talk to students about the style of illustrations, and which media will they use. Talking about whether to use crayons, chalk, watercolors, paper cutting, or other media will help them choose carefully and deliberately when planning for their illustrations.

Students now are ready to write and illustrate their published pieces. Be mindful of how long each student takes in this part of the process. More artistic students might spend too much time on the illustrations. Although publishing is an important part of the total writing experience, the learning is about writing, not illustrating, so make sure the student is moving along at a good pace is. Publishing is not just the culmination of the work, but the prize at the end of very complex and thoughtful work.

—◁◦◦▷—

PLANNING JOURNAL: YOUR THOUGHTS
ON PUBLISHING CONFERENCE

Planning for a successful publishing conference not only means thinking about what you will say to students, but it also involves where you will keep the publishing supplies. Think through some scenarios of publishing conferences. We like to keep stackable paper trays on the table so that the supplies are within reach of both teacher and student, but how you do this will depend on where you station yourself in the room. Consider which supplies your school has that you can use and any you might need to request.

A note about supplies: always ask before you purchase. It has been our experience that when asked for supplies, principals or parents provide them. Items such as brads, folders, or even cotton balls have shown up when asked for. We tend to forget to ask and, therefore, we take the autonomy out of the hands of those we seek to serve.

- What supplies will you need?
- Where will you keep the supplies used in the conference?
- How will you organize the supplies?
- What options will you have for students?
- Will you have students write on both sides of the page? Crayons work best. Paints or markers tend to bleed through the paper; then only one side of the paper may be used.
- Will you allow them to work on end pages (summary and author information)?
- What modes and materials will you allow students to use in their illustrations? Sometimes crayons are just fine; other times you may want to incorporate illustrator studies from reading or art lessons and have the students illustrate in that author's style.
- Will you have a special place for using special materials such as watercolor paints or pastel chalk?
- How much time will be necessary; and how much is too much when publishing?
- Which decisions will you make for students, and which decisions will they make for themselves? Use scaffolding and gradually turn the decisions over to students.

- Plan how you will use your mentor text to model a publishing conference. Show how you decide which text goes on each page and how you number the pages. Then decide what kind of book you will make.

Chapter Eleven

Publishing

This is where the writer puts it all together and makes the piece into something that can be shared. The piece becomes a real book that can be read. It isn't just that the book is "fancy" with a cover and pictures; it's that the piece has been worked on until it tells a good story, has no convention mistakes, the text is neat, and the pictures connect to the text. The book is the culmination of all of the hard work the student has put into it.

This view of the work is why it is important to write every day and publish every piece. Writers say to the world that they have something to say, and what they have to say is good. Students gain the confidence they need to push forward and improve their craft of writing. Writing and reading gain meaning. Publishing gives the students a purpose for their writing that then motivates them to make each book better than the previous one.

As their efficacy as a writer increases, they likely will begin to tackle writing with purpose, especially as they have experienced the piece becoming better over workshop time. Therefore, when a student takes an excessive amount of time to complete a piece, likely one of two things is occurring. First, the student is unsure what to do, even after a conference, or the writer is older and is writing longer pieces. Even if either of these is true, it is necessary that students publish more often, not less. Pieces that last four weeks, or pieces that last merely one day, do not allow the depth of processing and procedure that increase the writer's self-efficacy.

While a student works on publishing, he thinks about bringing the whole piece together into a cohesive work. He thinks about the design of the book, and his handwriting as he works to make it neat. He considers the illustrations to make sure they connect to the text to help convey meaning. He thinks about the page openings and the movement of the story. Most important, the student thinks about the experience the reader will have. All of this goes into the publishing process.

MENTOR TEXTS AND PUBLISHING

Using picture books in writing—in particular, showing illustrator craft—will help students to improve their own illustrations. Students can be shown how the text and the pictures work together to make a complete story. Choose a well-made picture book, cover the words with sticky notes, and type the words on plain white paper. Students look at the text by itself and look at the illustrations alone. Finally, have the students read the book complete with text and illustrations and talk about how the illustrations complete the text, telling a fuller story. A short picture book such as *Rosie's Walk* by Pat Hutchins (1968) works great; you can do that exercise in a five- to ten-minute mini-lesson. You can also use a book from a previous read aloud or reading lesson.

Getting students to look at the art in a picture book can increase their ability to use their own illustrations in a more connected way. Provide art materials and let students explore with a certain medium such as paper tearing or colored pencils. This can be done in an independent reading station once a week, or in collaboration with the art teacher, which allows connectivity across disciplines to happen without taking more classroom time. The important thing is to get the students to think deliberately about the publishing process.

Do an illustrator study with several texts, noting the illustrator's style, technique, and medium. After such a study, you may require students to make a book using that technique or medium. Note the illustrator's use of positive and negative space. How many things does each illustration contain? Does the illustration have a focus? Note the illustrator's use of color. Some illustrators use dull colors or grayscale, then suddenly switch to bright colors to emphasize a change in the story. In the book *Extra Yarn* by Mac Barnett (2012), only the yarn is in color; the rest of the illustrations are grayscale to show the power the yarn has on the town.

Look at covers, title pages, about the author sections, and dedications in picture books. Once students feel comfortable with the process and have published a few pieces, have them add some paratext in the published pieces.

It will enhance their thinking about text and publishing. You may want them to start with a title page for a few pieces. Then you can require that they all make a dedication page. When you feel the students are doing those well, you can require that they add an About the Author section to the back of the book. At first this section will be sparse, or contain unnecessary information. If you have students write one for each book and allow them to use the first one, you will find that they tweak and tighten the blurb about the author with each publishing.

Use your mentor text piece to show students the thinking that will happen as they publish. Making a book makes you a part of the writing community, but it also provides good information on the expectations during the publishing phase. Talk about how you might like an intricate illustration, but how you do not have enough time. Then decide on a less intricate illustration that works as well. Publishing should take no longer than the time it takes for students to work on each draft of their piece, usually one or two writing periods if the writing time is about forty minutes. Modeling how to make that happen can help the students be more productive with their time.

If you have an artisan in your midst, one you would like to allow some time to illustrate but know he often takes too long, time each page. The student uses the timer at his desk and is allowed a specific amount of time on each drawing. This will help him move along. Only use the timer when the amount of time seems problematic as the illustrating portion is an important part of the process of sharing and thinking deeply about the text.

When students go through the publishing process, they move to a new level of thinking about writing. No longer is the writing just for the teacher to grade. Now it is a way to make writing and reading come alive. Publishing helps students connect to the larger world and feel that they are a part of it as they connect to others in the world.

——◦◦◦——

PLANNING JOURNAL: YOUR THOUGHTS ON PUBLISHING

Most students love this part, so planning for it mainly involves recognizing the materials to be used and monitoring the use of time on task. Think about what will be available to the students, where materials will be stored, and how students will access them. Time on task with publishing results in the opposite of the problem you usually encounter in the classroom: students will be on task but may spend too much time drawing their illustrations. Setting parameters and allowing about the same time for publishing as for the other parts of the writing process is a rule of thumb. If students write a larger, more intricate piece, they might spend a bit more time in publishing as well. If they normally take two days to write a draft, then give them that much time to publish.

- Where will publishing supplies be kept for easy student access?
- Will you allow different mediums, or just one at time?
- Are there cleanup procedures?
- What are the time parameters for publishing?
- Plan the mini-lesson using your mentor text. What illustrations will you prepare ahead of time to talk about and which illustration will you work on during the mini-lesson to incorporate the metacognitive talk about making the book? Work on your book at this time, thinking about how you will structure this mini-lesson.

Chapter Twelve

Sharing

Students love to share their writing with the class, so setting aside a specific time to share gives students a protocol. It is the last five to ten minutes of writing workshop, and it should be a formal time with parameters set for both the reader and audience members. Sharing time provides the students with an authentic audience to write for when working through the process with their piece. This space creates a community around the writing practice. This community of practice allows students to experience trust from others while instilling a sense of accomplishment for themselves. A classroom's most valuable gift is this community, and writing workshop can instantiate it in profound ways.

In the first few days of writing workshop, no published works will be ready to share, so sharing a couple of works in progress each day is a good way to keep the others motivated to keep working. After about two weeks, generally one or two published pieces will be turned in each day for the rest of the year.

Sharing time is much more productive in teaching writing when published work rather than part of a draft is shared. The purpose of sharing published work is to let an audience enjoy the work, and students in the audience get to examine how others' published works look and sound. The purpose for sharing a work in progress is to gain insight into what revision a piece might need. Teacher and peer conferencing is a better venue for sharing works in progress.

WRITER AS READER PROTOCOL

The reader should have a special place to stand or sit as she shares, typically a read-aloud corner or carpeted space. Use a special author's chair, or use the teacher's chair, always a special place for students to be allowed to sit. Students in higher grades may want to read at the front of the class. Generally, a more intimate group makes the student feel more confident and the audiences more like listener-participants. The important part is to have a stable place where sharing occurs, and that the sharing is experienced as a celebration of a completed piece. Notice that we say *celebration*.

The author needs instruction in how to read a book aloud. Use mini-lessons to show students how to hold the book below the level of their faces so that their voices carry straight to the audience, unblocked by their book. Show them how to read the book straight on, then turn it around to show the audience the pictures. Show students how to move the pictures slowly across the audience's line of vision. Talk about how to speak up and speak clearly, precluding audience comment about not being able to hear while the author is reading. The goal is that the author need not stop sharing. When the sharing stops mid-read, the flow is disrupted. This disruption causes fluency, comprehension, and efficacy issues for the reader and for the listener, plus it simply takes too much time.

AUDIENCE PROTOCOL

Some students are shy and will not want to read their books to the class during sharing. Give these students two or three passes on sharing, or ask if you can read for them. Do let these students know that eventually they will have to read their pieces aloud to the class, so they can mentally prepare for that time. Have one-on-one conferences to encourage them gently and give helpful hints when the time comes, and even scaffold by reading it aloud with them either chorally or taking turns. Sharing teaches students about public speaking with material they are familiar with and can be read without having to memorize.

Sharing also helps fluency, comprehension, and phonological awareness for all children. The more they read aloud writing that they have composed, the better their reading will become. Their fluency and prosody become better as they read with more expression. When they read with more expression, both their comprehension and the audience's comprehension improve.

Sharing improves emergent or struggling readers' phonological awareness, as they must decode faster to keep up a smooth reading cadence.

The key to successful sharing with all students, though, lies with the audience. The audience needs to be taught how to be good listeners and good responders. This is a great time to teach politeness, positivity, and compassion. Listening quietly is not easy for children when the person speaking, typically an inexperienced or quiet reader, does not command the room. Teaching students that it is rude to interrupt or have a side conversation when a classmate is reading her book helps them learn to be better audience members. In addition, students learn to be more compassionate when they are reminded that they will be reading their books to the whole class in the future.

In order to stay within the time frame of five to ten minutes, have the reader choose only two people to comment on the piece. The comments are always positive; students say what they liked and why they liked it. Critical review of the piece lies with the teacher during the conferences and grading. Sharing time is a positive time where the students can relish their accomplishment and feel proud of their work.

All of these protocols and rules bring the class to a situation in which kindness, compassion, and civility create an atmosphere of connectivity and acceptance to the classroom community. Thus, all students, but shy students especially, are more willing to share because they know they will be accepted, and the experience will be a positive one. Making students comfortable with the process will increase their work ethic and improve their social skills.

Teachers are active people watchers. We love talking to students and watching them interact with each other. In this case, sharing time will be especially interesting to you. When the first students finish publishing and begin to share, the audience is transformed. Within the first few weeks of writing workshop, reluctant writers are still very skeptical about the whole process. Whether they do not think they can be successful or they just do not think they can finish a piece, seeing others publish and share has a very magical quality to it. Once they see that others in the class are publishing, and that it looks and sounds good, they are hooked. All of a sudden, they believe they can be successful writers, too, and will work hard to publish their current piece. Sharing provides an impetus to finishing that all-important first piece.

Sharing also gives the audience ideas for topics they can write about. If one student writes about her best friend, other students see that they can write about their best friends. Sometimes it gives a student a jumping-off place for coming up with another topic he might write about. If one student writes a piece about basketball, then another student might write about dancing. Sharing gives students so many good ideas that writer's block is not really an issue once momentum in the process is going strong.

A great way to teach all of the aspects of sharing time is to read your published mentor text to the students. As you read, explain the procedure and use metacognitive talk about what you are doing as a reader. For audience instruction, have a good reader read a short book to the class and use metacognitive talk about what a good audience does and what questions are best to ask. These discussions and descriptions can be mini-lessons that you teach during the first few sharing times before anyone has published his first piece.

Sharing is the culmination of a job well done. It will happen every one or two weeks for each student, reinforcing learning that has taken place during the writing process. This frequent encouragement provides momentum for the work students do as writers. When students share, they are motivated to work harder on the next piece. This is why going through the entire process for every piece is so valuable for the students.

———⟡⟡⟡———

PLANNING JOURNAL: YOUR THOUGHTS ON SHARING

You will want your sharing time to run smoothly, quickly, and create a strong sense of classroom community. How you run it will make a huge difference in bringing about all of these things. Plan your sharing time by considering all of the details that need to be orchestrated.

- Where will sharing take place?
- Where will the author sit or stand?
- Where will the audience sit?
- What will the transition look like? How will you get students to put away their writing for the day and get to the sharing place quickly and quietly?
- What will you teach about sharing a published piece?

- What will your expectations be for each student (loudness, presentation style, time)? Think about specific students. For example, shy students or behaviorally disruptive students might require particular decision-making. How will you scaffold the process of getting the shy student to share? When a child is disruptive, what will be the consequence? How will you make sure that the audience is quiet for the reader?
- What types of comments should be made and how should they be framed?
- How many comments will you allow to make sure you do not run out of time?
- How will you help the class be civil, polite, and kind to each other?
- Plan how you will model both the reading and audience behavior using your own mentor text.

Part II

Putting It All Together

Chapter Thirteen

Mini-Lessons and Mentor Texts

Many teachers think of a lesson cycle as a presentation to the whole class, followed by guided practice wherein the teacher asks questions to determine understanding, ending with some independent practice, usually a worksheet or writing prompt that will be graded and recorded in the grade book. The problem with these whole-group lessons is that students retain very little of what is presented, usually because the teacher talks for twenty minutes or more.

The questioning is largely ineffective because the students who answer are the top students who do understand with little instruction. This leaves out the quiet students and those who won't raise their hands because they don't understand. If a teacher calls on the student she knows might not understand in an attempt to model for others a clearer understanding, most students tune out as the answer gets complicated and wordy. Even if the teacher questioned every student, would the question be the right one to check for that student's understanding?

This is key to many of the problems in our classrooms. Instruction must be monitored, and whole-class questioning is not a way to do so. Acquiring depth of understanding of a skill without authentic, personal practice is difficult, if not impossible. The worksheet is usually practice of a particular skill in isolation, which will not carry over into authentic or even prompt writing. If this lesson cycle is ineffective, how can we design lessons to create authentic learning that creates better writers who love to write?

Whole-group mini-lessons coupled with individual conferences can provide the instruction that encourages writers and pushes them forward in their craft. Mini-lessons are essentially the teacher talking to the whole class, but only for five to ten minutes. In this short time, a teacher has to explain the concept clearly and efficiently, showing the students how it works in authentic writing. The mini-lesson has to be precise because it can be no longer than ten minutes, as most students start tuning out after that time. It allows no time to check for understanding through questions to the whole class, but that is OK because checks for understanding happen during individual conferences. Think of the lesson as a short explanation or demonstration. What do students need to know at this time in their writing progression? Explain the concept succinctly, giving only the necessary information.

You can use a visual or take notes to provide a resource for the students later and reinforce your explanation, but stay within ten minutes. Remember not to ask any questions; however, students can ask you questions for clarification during the mini-lesson. Because students are used to teachers talking and questioning for longer periods of time, it will take them a while to get used to this quick, precise information. Soon they will really focus on the lesson once they know you won't talk more than ten minutes and they will need the information to use in their pieces. Their attention will be heightened because the lesson is so pertinent to their work.

Students also will pay more attention to the mini-lessons because they know you will ask them about previous content during a conference if they do not use the construct correctly. In traditional whole-group questioning, students were able to stay under the radar. Now they will be called on to know and use the information because the questioning will be individual and specific to the piece.

When you confer with a student, peruse the piece of writing for misunderstandings, particularly within the concepts you have taught, and ask the student questions about different aspects of the piece. Questioning and reteaching happen in a conference, tailoring instruction specifically for each student. If needed, you can call a small group for a short reteach when you see four or five students having the same issue, not the whole class, and not just a couple.

Mini-lessons are used to introduce and reinforce all aspects of the writing craft. Any lesson done under the language arts umbrella can be taught in a mini-lesson. Any writing standard can be taught in a mini-lesson. You can cover it all in mini-lessons. The trick is learning how to present new information or revisit material concisely in five to ten minutes. If the concept seems too large to fit in that time, break it into smaller chunks of information and present it in a series of mini-lessons over several days.

For example, your scope and sequence requires that you teach figurative language. On the first day, you might give an overview of figurative language by showing good writers using it to enhance their pieces. On days two and three, you might look specifically at metaphor and onomatopoeia. Students will gain more from these small presentations: each offers less to remember and think about, the explanation is clear, and topics can be revisited to reinforce previous learning.

ANCHOR CHARTS AND NOTES

Because mini-lessons are so concise and short, it can be a good idea to give the students a resource to help them remember the concepts. Anchor charts and notes can provide resources that students can access during their writing when they have questions or need information. These should be organized in a way that helps students find just the information they need when they need it, quickly and easily and without you having to remind them.

Storing notes and small paper anchor charts in a special place in students' notebooks with tabs makes it easier for them to find the information. Large anchor charts should be placed on the wall in categories to help the students find the information fast. The quicker they can access the information, the more likely they are to use the notes and anchor charts.

Anchor charts are large charts that are hung around the room and used as quick resources for information when needed. They provide a visual representation for your mini-lessons, and they are great resources and reminders of mini-lessons. As quick resources, anchor charts should be clear and precise, just like your mini-lessons, containing very little text and only one or two connected ideas based on the mini-lesson.

When students ask a question answerable on an anchor chart, you only have to tell them to use their resources and leave it up to them to find the information. Because they need the information, they will look for it. Once they have been reminded a few times and know that you will not give them the answer, they will begin to look for the resource before they ask you. They will become more independent writers.

If you search Google for anchor charts and click images, a plethora of anchor charts pop up, most of them done badly because they are too wordy. If a student who struggles in reading has to read a lot of text, he won't use the anchor chart. Anchor charts are meant to be *quick* resources to look at, connect to their writing, and apply within a few moments. In other words, anchor charts need to be user friendly. If they are too much trouble, students won't use them, and therefore they won't learn the information.

Anchor charts should have fewer than twenty-five words, and if you can make an anchor chart with fewer than ten words, so much the better. This will make the information easy to find, easy to understand, and easy to use. Using graphics, such as boxes, arrows, or symbolic pictures, to connect the text on the anchor chart helps organize and point out the useful information. Making charts more pictorial helps the students understand the information more efficiently and be more likely to use it.

Look at print ads on the Internet or in magazines. The company wants you first to notice the ad and then internalize its message. Huge amounts of research have been done to get people to do these two things. Ads have some type of graphic and a few bold words. We know that concept works because people buy the stuff that ads sell. The ads do not tell everything about the product; they tell you what you need to know to buy the product and make buying the product more desirable. A well-made anchor chart has the same effect: its few bold words and a graphic lead the reader to the important message. Once students find the process of using resources helps their writing, they are more likely to use them in the future.

Although anchor charts hang on the wall, they don't need to stay there all year. Rotate anchor charts on and off the wall as needed. Say you make an anchor chart about periods, question marks, and exclamation marks, and you hang it on the wall for a resource. Once you see that most of students have mastered that skill, take down that chart, leaving room for a new one. Too many anchor charts on the wall makes it harder for students to find the information they need. Keep the anchor chart wall clutter-free, as a more sparse design will help students access the materials.

Notes can be another resource for students. Taking notes helps students internalize the information. Writing out the notes slows the process of getting new information, whereas hearing new information only takes a few seconds. When listening to a lecture, students have but a few seconds to process information before the teacher moves on to the next piece of information. When writing out notes, the students have a few minutes to process new information while they focus on writing it down, making them able to more fully internalize the new information.

Taking notes can be difficult for students if they have had little experience with it or are very young, so placing the information on the board or document camera for them to copy gives them experience in concise note-taking. Think of taking notes as a process to be learned. First, students need to see you taking notes, which they can copy exactly into their notebooks. The younger the students, the more experience they need in copying your notes. Once they have enough of that experience, you can scaffold note-taking by telling students the information once. Tell them they will need to make their own notes, then repeat the information. The students then write their own notes.

The next step is to have them share their notes with another student. This sharing allows students to see how other students organize the information, giving them more ideas on how to organize information in their own notes. Only after much experience in taking notes like this are students ready to take notes independently as you present information. Because the concept of taking notes involves listening, then writing down their understanding, students usually don't reach the independent stage until third grade or later. Continuing the note-taking experience with copying and/or sharing is good experience for students in kindergarten through second grade. When they are ready cognitively to take notes independently, they will.

Just like anchor charts, notes should be concise—a few words that give meaning to the concept and can be used as a resource when needed. Graphic organizers, bullet lists, visuals, and outlines work great for this purpose. Have students write these notes with organization; it helps them retain and make sense of the information, which is the goal of taking notes. Graphically organized notes help the brain connect and process the information. Students might remember the information later, or at least remember that they did something with the information they need and know where to find it. Either way students won't ask you for the information, which frees your time for conferences.

Handouts can be made with information organized in the same manner as anchor charts or notes. Make them simple and concise for easy access to the information. Make copies of the handouts on half sheets of paper so they fit onto a page in the notebook for easy reference. Students can tape or glue the handout into a specific section of the notebook. Leave blanks in the handout for students to fill in as a scaffold for taking notes. Give students a few minutes to think about the information and process it. This will help them remember the information enough to know where to find it when they need it.

Plan ahead. Give deep thought to your notes, handouts, and anchor charts. Think about exactly what information students might need, and when. Then design the notes, handouts, or anchor charts to fit that need. They will save you from repeating and reteaching concepts while moving students to become more responsible in their own work.

MENTOR TEXTS

A mentor text is a piece of good writing the teacher uses in a mini-lesson. Because good writers use all of the concepts and conventions of quality writing, showing good examples gives students ideas for how to use concepts correctly in their own writing. A good mentor text can teach the students many things about writing in a paragraph or a page. Students can learn about good hooks or beginnings, good endings, descriptive writing, dialogue, transitions, first- and third-person point of view, as well as all of the conventions used in each type of writing. Literally thousands of good books are available to illustrate any number of concepts, providing thousands of good teachers for your students to learn from.

Finding good mentor texts is fun. Set aside time to read, and you will be surprised to find out how much you enjoy combing literature for quality writing examples. Finding mentor texts means reading like a writer—looking at the word choice, the sentence variety, examples of conventional structures, and other aspects of the writer's craft. Continue to read for enjoyment, and as you do, keep an eye out for that great sentence, good paragraph, or extraordinary use of adjectives. Your curriculum guide might offer example mentor texts, but be sure to read them beforehand; one you choose might not showcase the skill or knowledge you think it does and, more important, you might have one that you and your students would like better that will do the same thing!

Using a book from your reading lesson that provides an example of a skill is also an idea. This allows time for a quick lesson as students already are engaged with the text. Remember, you need not necessarily read the whole text to showcase an example. Sometimes reading a small portion of a new text is sufficient. Texts you start but do not complete make great additions to kids' reading lists. With a bit of encouragement, students will want to read the rest of the story themselves.

Teacher Writing as a Mentor Text

Kelly Gallagher (2011) tells us that we are the best writers in the class. This is true no matter what age your students are. As adults, teachers, and college graduates, we can write at a much higher level than our students. Occasionally we get a gifted writer in our class, but she will not have the writing experience you have. Not only are we the best writers, but we are the best teachers in our classes. Therefore, our writing can be great mentor texts.

Students need to see their teachers as writers. Sharing the writing experience with your students helps them understand the process better. Using your writing in mini-lessons gives them valuable insight into how writers think while they are writing. You can model any aspect of writing, with the added bonus of getting inside a writer's head. Whether the writing is done on a computer or longhand with a document camera, the teacher can think aloud as the writing is happening, showing the students the choices and struggles that are a natural part of the writing process. Students need to see that struggle, connecting what happens inside their heads to what ends up on the paper. They need to learn that struggling with the writing will help them to become good writers, because many good writers struggle.

In the first part of this book, we asked you to go through the writing process and write a piece to be used as a mentor text. This mentor text is a great tool for the students. Re-create this mentor text as you go through the process in front of the students. Think out loud as you write, revise, confer, edit, and publish your piece. This piece of writing will be more valuable to students' sense of writing than a published book by a famous author because students will see how an author writes and thinks while writing, and thus will get examples of the work and struggle in the process. If you have not written this mentor text, stop now and go through the process of writing it to use in mini-lessons.

Any and every part of the writing process can be a mini-lesson, so writing in front of your students will help them understand how a writer collects, organizes, drafts, revises, edits, publishes, and shares. The mini-lesson needs to stop at ten minutes, so you will only be able to write part of a piece, all that the students need to see to understand the specific part of the writing process. Finish the draft or revision on your own and have the piece ready for the next mini-lesson on the next step in the process. Conferring with yourself about your own writing gives students ideas for self-talk they can use after they finish a draft and when they are waiting for a conference with you. Modeling conferences teaches the students to think through their pieces with a writer's eye.

Using your own texts as mentor texts gives the students information about writing that no other text can. It is personal because it is your text, and the students can see your inner struggle and hear your inner talk, then transfer that thinking to their own work. Throughout this process, the teacher ceases to be the keeper of knowledge and becomes the sharer of writing strategies— strategies that your students can and will use in their own writing.

Picture Books as Mentor Texts

Picture books have a strong text-to-illustration connection in storytelling; however, because the text is usually minimal, using picture books shows students how to get their point across with precision. Picture books are useful for mini-lessons on word choice, sentence structure, story leads, story endings, punctuation, capitalization, story focus, text to illustration connections, and many other aspects of writing.

Using mentor texts that have extraordinary leads that can be emulated easily can help young writers. *Lilly's Purple Plastic Purse* by Kevin Henkes (1996) is a good example. It starts with a broad statement, "Lilly loved school," then details why Lilly loved school. This type of lead can be a good way for students to begin stories if they are making poor choices, such as what they ate for breakfast or jumping right into the story. Showing good leads in mini-lessons and pointing out why they are good will connect with many of your students.

It's OK if students copy the structure of a good piece of writing. They aren't copying the writing; they are following the way a quality author used words and sentences. This gives them practice in forming structures of writing. When students try the structures in their own writing, those structures are internalized. Then they become the jumping-off point for creating students' own structures.

Because students like to publish with illustrations, use picture books to show how pictures enhance or connect to the story. Pictures in student work can be two dimensional and flat, often only showing one aspect of the writing on the page. Show students how pictures and text match up in more complex ways.

For example, illustrations usually show the characters' emotions in ways that are at once clear and connective to the reader. Novice writers often leave out how a person felt or reacted to an event in their writing, so having them add those emotional ties through their illustrations can help them convey the message as well as help the students to see the need for emotions in stories. This is also a bridge to writing about those emotions in their texts. Once students understand the picture-text connection more deeply, they begin to show those same aspects in their own work, first trying the demonstrated concepts and later branching out, trying new ideas in the scaffolds of others and finally on their own.

Novels as Mentor Texts

Novels are a rich source of sample writing. Excerpts can show ways in which writing moves and flows from one sentence to another, from one paragraph to another. They can show description and use of adjectives, pronouns, verbs, and nouns. Novels are an excellent source of the use of dialogue, noting how characters talk to one another, the purpose of dialogue in the story, and the punctuation that accompanies it. Novel passages are great ways to show conventions in writing and how punctuation or word choice is used in different contexts.

Passages from novels work best when students are familiar with the story; however, a well-chosen passage can double as a hook to get students to read the book on their own while still teaching a mini-lesson on an aspect of writing. In this situation you can use books above the students' reading level, as their listening comprehension level always is higher than their reading comprehension level. Plan what and when you want to teach through a piece of a novel so it works well as a mini-lesson.

Novels provide great examples of descriptive writing. In *Tuck Everlasting* (1975), Natalie Babbitt's description in the first paragraph invokes a clear image of a hot August day. The stifling heat bears down on the reader, connecting her to the story right away. The goal is not for your students to write like Natalie Babbitt, but rather to add description that *shows* the reader rather than *tells* the reader. In the same way, using novels in mini-lessons shows young writers how to write well.

Sometimes students have seen a popular movie made from a book but have not read the book. Passages from these books make good mentor texts as the students already are familiar with the story's plot. Using text from these books can give students an impetus to read the book on their own and can aid in their comprehension. As most readers say, "The book is way better than the movie," you are providing an avenue for students to decide this on their own.

Connecting Reading to Writing with Mentor Texts

Most mentor texts cannot be read in their entirety in ten minutes, which creates a dilemma with familiarity. Although we want students to love reading and writing, and to enjoy lots of stories completely, a mini-lesson is not the time to do this. Mini-lessons only use pieces of text from a picture book or novel. Read these books in their entirety before the mini-lesson, or introduce a new text in a mini-lesson. Then it acts not only as a mentor text, but also as a book talk to interest students in reading it on their own.

Reading these texts for pleasure the first time lets students enjoy the moments of being absorbed in a story and savor it. If students only read for assignments where the writing is picked apart for vocabulary or main idea, they will never come to enjoy reading. Reading mentor texts ahead of time allows students to enjoy the book so they can recall the text, the art, and the themes later during a mini-lesson. Use guided reading time or read-aloud times to share mentor texts before the texts become mini-lessons. Using books for reading before they become mentor texts for writing gives students the opportunity to read like a reader.

Once they have read a text like a reader, they are ready to read the text like a writer, combing through details for examples they can transfer to their own writing. Texts can be enjoyed as the students can learn to understand and comprehend the text in its fullness. Once they have enjoyed the text, it is ready to be dissected for the writing concepts it contains.

Although texts can be read during guided reading instruction, story times or read-aloud times are best to enjoy future mentor texts. Students can just listen and enjoy a good story or nonfiction book. When the text then is used in a mini-lesson, students are familiar with it and can focus on the part you highlight in the mini-lesson as a good piece of writing.

Plan your mentor texts. They can even be introduced and read months before they are used in mini-lessons. The goal for using texts in mini-lessons during writer's workshop is that they showcase the exact knowledge or skill you are teaching. Thus, it is OK to show multiple examples of that skill through multiple texts without feeling the need to teach whole texts. Remember, this is not an exercise in comprehension of text per se, but an overt example of a quality piece of writing.

Responding to Mentor Texts

Sometimes you will read a mentor text to students and then have students respond in any way they choose. It can be a particularly descriptive piece of writing, or invoke thinking about a big idea. This exercise serves several purposes. Maybe you want students to listen and absorb the way in which the author wrote. The response can be writing about what they think about the author's ideas, or the way the author chose to write about the topic. The response can be about the author's use of metaphor, or adjectives, or any other writing device.

Whatever the purpose, it should be a quick write. Use only a few minutes to read the passage, allowing about five minutes for the students to respond in writing. As the mini-lesson for the day, the activity should take no more than ten minutes. This exercise helps students think about writing in new ways. It also helps them write through some initial thoughts more quickly; in turn, it helps them compose first drafts quickly by getting their thoughts down on the page.

Mini-Lessons on Conventions

Conventions are rules that writers need to follow so readers can easily understand the writing. They don't bring meaning to the writing, but they help convey the meaning. Think about the last vacation you took. You had to take a car, a train, or an airplane to reach your destination. The method of transportation was not your vacation; it only helped you get to your vacation. Conventions aren't the writing, but they help others enjoy the writing. Many times, we treat conventions as if they are the reason to write. Although conventions are important, they are only a small part of learning to write well. Keep this in perspective as you plan mini-lessons.

Having students correct sentences that are written incorrectly tends to reinforce the incorrect structure rather than teach the correct structure (Godley, Carpenter, and Werner, 2007). Therefore, teaching conventions through well-written mentor texts can empower students to use conventions within their own writing. Seeing how quality writing uses conventions provides students with a better construct for how conventions work and when to use them. Using mentor texts (including your own writing) shows students the correct ways real authors use them within authentic pieces of writing.

Many children's books explain conventions in fun and informative ways, such as the book series by Brian P. Cleary that plays with words. Cleary's books such as *A Mink, a Fink, a Skating Rink: What Is a Noun?* (1999) can be used to learn about different parts of speech. Remember, the goal is that your students use conventions in their own writing. Merely reading a good story and pointing out conventions will not achieve this; use conferences to create a bridge between the story and the correct usage of the convention. A good writing teacher shows many examples and refers to mentor texts when conferring about these skills. This promotes autonomy in students' writing. Mentor texts will become reference materials, much like the anchor charts that accumulate over time.

Mini-Lessons on Spelling

Students often let the spelling of a word bring their writing to a screeching halt. Help them internalize your permission to sound out a word in the drafting and revising stages. It is hard at first, but it will help them to move through the process more smoothly and give them confidence in their writing. Spelling corrections can and should be done in the editing stage of the process, because spelling a word correctly helps the reader comprehend the piece.

Older students will hesitate, even balk at the notion of having a word spelled wrong on their paper. As they age, they know it is wrong but not how to remedy it. Giving them a strategy, such as circling a word they know is spelled wrong, enables them to feel as if they are capable of knowing but need a facilitator to bridge their experiential gap.

You may wonder about the common traditional practice of learning weekly spelling words that culminate in a weekly spelling test. Forget about it. As teachers, each of us has had experience with a high-ability student who comes for an editing conference on Monday with a word from the previous week's spelling test misspelled, even when he received 100 percent on the spelling test! If a student who consistently scores high on her spelling tests cannot correctly transfer the spelling word to her writing, then the way that we "teach" spelling does not work. Why spend valuable classroom time on something that does not work?

Instead, use mini-lessons and conferences (as well as frequent reading) to spur students to spell words correctly. Mini-lessons can focus on spelling patterns in the same way many spelling books focus their weekly lessons. You can even use the weekly lists from spelling books to design mini-lessons. Make mini anchor charts with words that fit into a specific spelling pattern. Having a spelling mini-lesson each week will help you keep up with the spelling patterns that the students need to learn.

Make word lists with these spelling patterns and hang them on the walls as anchor charts, or place them in students' writing folders as a reference guide. Word walls will help students remember the spelling and meaning as well as give them choices of words to use in their writing. The more students use these word walls, the easier and more automatic the spelling becomes.

As new word walls are made, older ones can be taken down. So the words students learn to spell changes throughout the year, and they are held accountable for the learning that has taken place. Use a section of your wall for these word walls so students automatically know where to look, and word walls can stay for several weeks until you replace them. Replacing old words with new ones promotes learning, as the students know the word wall is temporary, and they will work harder to remember the patterns. You can have students copy the words on the anchor chart into their notebooks before you take it down so that they will still have them as a resource. Your word work in writing must change to aid in use.

In addition, using high-frequency word lists created by researchers such as Edward Dolch help you recognize words that students read and write frequently and thus, should grasp methodically. During conferences, notice which words are giving students trouble. Plan mini-lessons on spelling these high-frequency words. Make anchor charts or handouts of these words for students' easy access to the information after the mini-lesson.

Mini-Lessons on Spell Check

If your classroom contains enough computers for students to write on them regularly, then the issue of spell check arises. Students know about spell check and will use it—inappropriately. Spell check is great if the person has a fairly good command of how spelling works in standard English. If not, students will end up with sentences that don't make sense because they picked the first word on the list.

Mini-lessons on how to choose the word a writer wants to use can help students develop a strategy for using spell check. Stand behind a student using a computer and show her your spell-check strategy step-by-step. Select the word in question and read each word on the list (usually students don't do that). If the word she wants is on the list, then choose that one. If the word is not there, point the student back to her original word and have her spell it again, sounding it out. Asking another student for the first three letters can help her get a list with the word she wants. The key to using spell check is to come as close to the correct spelling as possible. If students don't find the word after several tries, have them deal with it during the editing conference.

The red squiggle underline can remind students the word is spelled incorrectly and needs to be worked on later. You can teach students to turn off the spell-check function in Word that shows spelling mistakes if it bothers them too much. They can turn it on right before editing conference to help them find misspelled words. Used correctly, spell check can become a lifelong aid to doing searches on the computer. Choosing the first item on a list seems inherent for novice computer users, whether within their writing or Web browsing. Writing in a Word document can aid their writing on a computer, a skill they can apply more broadly as they grow.

Mini-Lessons on Punctuation and Capitalization

Mini-lessons on punctuation and capitalization can use just about any passage from any text because they are found in every good piece of writing. Now and then you will run across a paragraph from a mentor text that has terrific examples of the use of a specific punctuation. The following from *The House on Mango Street* by Sandra Cisneros (1991, 6) is an example of such a featured punctuation: "My papa's hair is like a broom, all up in the air. And me, my hair is lazy. It never obeys barrettes or bands. Carlos's hair is thick and straight. He doesn't need to comb it."

This paragraph shows the use of apostrophes in possessives in "papa's hair." In the phrase, "Carlos's hair," it also shows how the writer used an "apostrophe s" with a possessive after a name ending with an "s." It shows students how apostrophes work in contractions as well with the word "doesn't." This paragraph shows the use of plurals and how they get either an "s" or "es," which many students confuse with possessives, and thus will put "'s" at the end of a plural. Paragraphs such as this with great examples of punctuation and capitalization are in any great piece of literature for use during mini-lessons.

Mini-Lessons on Parts of Speech

Teaching nouns, verbs, adjectives, and adverbs seems easy. Put the lesson in the context of real writing, or it will not transfer very well. Teaching what an adjective is and showing its use in writing gives students ideas for using adjectives in their own writing, but they must use and identify these parts of speech in their writing and others' to understand what they are and how to use them authentically.

Using a piece of your writing, show students how to find and highlight the nouns in their writing. In another mini-lesson, take that draft with the nouns underlined or highlighted and model how to reread sentences to determine whether they need an adjective before the noun. Writing in which an adjective precedes every noun is cumbersome. Modeling aloud how a writer chooses an adjective, or not, gives students a better idea of when to add one.

This type of mini-lesson is also helpful to English language learners because it explicitly showcases how parts of speech work to create meaning in standard English. Rules—for example, an adjective coming before the noun it modifies—are important to explicate because not all languages have the same structures. The goal of any lesson about parts of speech is to help students construct better sentences, not necessarily to identify nouns and adjectives.

Mini-Lessons on Subject-Verb Agreement

Once students are writing more complex sentences, they may have some trouble with subject-verb agreement, making the noun match the verb and knowing when to put an "s" at the end of a verb. In more complex sentence structures, prepositional phrases may be added to the noun in the subject before the verb. In this construction, the students might match the verb to the prepositional phrase instead of to the noun that is the actual subject. For example, a student wrote, "The cats in the basket watches the wind-up toy mouse." Here, "cats" is the subject and thus, the verb needs to be "watch," but the student confused the prepositional phrase "in the basket" as the subject and used "watches" instead. Showing pieces of quality mentor texts that highlight how subject-verb agreement works can help students figure out subject-verb agreement in their writing during the composing, revising, and editing stages. It also allows teachers to point students to read good examples the class has covered previously.

Mini-Lessons on Tenses

Students often mix the tenses in their writing because they write as they would speak. Although orally they move between present and past tense, in writing we maintain one tense. For example, "He is going to the store and got us candy." We recognize what the writer is saying orally, but it is incorrect in writing. Use your own piece where you have mixed the tenses as a mentor text. Let students see as you talk about your thinking while you circle the verbs, decide which tense to use, and change verbs so that the tense matches throughout to give students a process to work through in their own pieces.

Comparing mentor texts that use present tense with pieces that use past tense can help students determine which tense is appropriate for their own piece. The purpose of working on tenses is to make the students' writing flow more smoothly and read more easily. Reading text that flip-flops between present and past tense brings a dissonance that makes it hard to read.

Plan a mini-lesson that focuses on why it is important for students to learn the concept of tenses. The answer always should be to help students become better writers. If the answer is something different, then maybe students don't need to learn it. If this reason for the lesson is your focus, then making your mini-lessons purposeful is easy.

A mentor text is any text that shows quality writing; this can be a published work or your own piece. Whether you are teaching students how to write a good lead or how to punctuate a sentence with a list, mentor texts serve as positive role models for novice writers. Reading children's literature, whether picture books or novels, is the best way to find great mentor texts and gives your students momentum to read. Remember, you are the best writer in the class, and using your writing as mentor texts shows students the work and the struggle that goes into good writing.

The key to a good mini-lesson: keep it under ten minutes and make it clear and to the point, focused on why students need to understand the concept your are teaching. By looking at students' writing, you will improve at this over time as you reflect on the process and evaluate what the students got from a mini-lesson. Gauging the mini-lesson by the changes you see in students' writing helps you create really good mini-lessons.

—⌇⌇⌇—

PLANNING JOURNAL: YOUR THOUGHTS ON MINI-LESSONS AND MENTOR TEXTS

Planning for mini-lessons is the main way to plan for writing workshop on a weekly basis. To start, think about the concepts in your scope and sequence. Begin with those lessons and think about how to restructure them into mini-lessons. Most curriculums have lessons that are too long and require little of the learner. Your lessons ask students to engage in the task as writers, not merely answer a series of questions.

Maybe set aside a certain day of the week for mini-lessons on conventions, so it is a constant part of your lesson strategy and meets the sequence of the English language arts and reading curriculum. For instance, Tuesdays you would always teach a mini-lesson on punctuation, capitalization, parts of speech and sentence construction, and Thursdays you would always look at spelling patterns. The other three days you would offer mini-lessons on other aspects of the writing process or the attributes of a genre of writing.

The first mini-lessons are extremely important; they set up the structure of writing workshop and set the tone for learning and working in that structure. Write a series of mini-lessons to help students understand how writing workshop works and how they will work within this structure.

- How will you introduce writing workshop on the first day?
- Will you have a mini-lesson on procedures in the classroom?
- Will you have mini-lessons on each part of the writing process, or teach it as a holistic, recursive approach?
- Will you use the mentor text you wrote in part I? What will those mini-lessons look like, and how many mini-lessons will you need? If you didn't compose this mentor text following the writing process, do it now.

Now make an overall plan for the mini-lessons you want to teach during the year. A mini-lesson needs a mentor text, an anchor chart, a handout or student notes. It might have two of those, but it will not have all of those things in one mini-lesson. List the concepts you need to teach. For each concept, decide the following:

- How often will you give a mini-lesson on this concept? When?
- Will you use a mentor text for this lesson? Will you use your own writing or a published book? Which one?
- Will you need an anchor chart? Sketch it.
- Will you give a handout? Sketch it.
- Will students write notes from your mini-lessons? What will they look like?

Chapter Fourteen

Teacher Conferences

This is where the majority of teaching and student learning happens. Writing workshop is the embodiment of one-on-one differentiation. Mini-lessons provide instruction to the whole group on concepts everyone in that age group and grade level needs. Teacher conferences provide exact instruction for each individual child, particular to the child's development as a writer and reader. Even though these conferences are short and to the point, they are powerful and will be internalized because you are teaching and reinforcing something specific using the student's own writing.

The goal is to keep your conferences to less than five minutes. Although a five-minute conference seems short, think of the target age and students' ability to follow directions and stay attuned. Think about the students' ability to remember the conversation and use notes to change multiple aspects of their pieces. A first grader will remember and attend to about three revisions; a fifth grader may be able to make more than six revisions. Long conferences or conferences with directions that are too plentiful leave students confused about what they need to work on. The result may be that a student only does the items the teacher mentions and does not think about how to use the skills he has been taught. As teachers, we want to avoid this learned helplessness, especially in writing, which requires much time and effort.

At first it will be difficult to confer in less than five minutes. Don't beat yourself up when it lasts longer. You are learning how to hold conferences effectively, and you haven't mastered it—yet. But you will. As you get better and better, you will find your rhythm and cadence and know which students need the full time, and which might not. Then conferencing will be like conducting an orchestra, directing each student while the writing class as a whole runs smoothly. At first you may want to time yourself using your phone or the wall clock. Don't set an alarm, though; just let it be, check your time at the end, and work faster in the next conference.

After everyone has completed a few pieces, you will know each student as a writer. You will know when the conference starts what each student needs to work on, so your teaching for that piece of writing will move toward improving the writing in those particular ways, differentiated for the needs of each student. The more experience you gain with conferring, the faster you will work and the more you will know about your students as writers. You will improve naturally.

If you confer about the organizer, look over it and ask students questions about why they put the subtopics where they did. Would they fit somewhere else? Did the student leave out something? Does the piece have too many subtopics, and could the student delete some of them?

Revision conferences will be the longest. Listen to the student read, then give thoughtful advice. Don't take shortcuts here; how a student revises will determine how well the paper is written. The goal is to help the piece become better. Ask yourself, "What does this piece need to be more cohesive and comprehensible?" In addition, think about the student's skills and how you can raise them to the next level.

If the piece is short or average in length, think about what is missing. Does the story have gaps? Is there something you don't quite understand? Ask the student these questions and listen to her answer. Then jot down a word or phrase in the margin near the place the new information belongs to help her to remember to add it in as you explain why that information will help the piece. When she rewrites, she will make her own decisions about where to add the information and will compose a new sentence for the piece.

If the piece is more than a couple of pages, it probably is too long. Listen to the first few paragraphs and scan the rest. Steer the student toward making it shorter by focusing on the center of the story. Ask questions about the point of the piece and listen to the answers to determine how to direct the student. Then jot down the focus at the top of the page. Have the student make cuts by crossing out information that doesn't connect to the theme. Focus so that the student is making the cuts, not you. If need be, students can return for another short conference about their additions or deletions.

If the student needs a better beginning, offer two options he could use to interest the reader from the start. Use a previous mentor text as an example, or parts of the student's text to bring the focus or point to the front of the piece. When looking at the body of the text to find a good start, have the student state that point clearly and write it at the top of the page. Ask the student what simple statement about the topic readers could relate to and agree on. What he says can be written verbatim or as a phrase above the point written down previously. Have the student start with those ideas to make the beginning more interesting. The student can then work it into the beginning.

If the student needs to work on the ending, have her first rephrase the point of the piece. Write this at the bottom of the piece. Then have her think about why this matters to her peers or to the world in general. Write down the answer, or an important phrase from the answer. Have her start with the point and work it in in a way that ends with the "so what?" of the piece. You are scaffolding the techniques or the structures of a good beginning or ending so students can recompose those parts.

In editing conferences you read sentence by sentence, silently or out loud. Explain the need for each correction. Although you explain each sentence, you can move and talk fast. The student generally gets it because you speak specifically about his writing. The text is familiar because the student has now written it twice. Only now is attention readily paid to the editing. Teachers and students often get caught up in editing because novice writers make so many mistakes. Avoid that worry. Know that in the end, students will think about conventions and the writing will be edited correctly.

After one or two of these face-to-face editing conferences, you can take a shortcut to save time. At the end of the period a few students will be waiting to have a conference with you. Ask what kind of conference they need. If students need an editing conference, take their folders and set them aside. At the end of the day, pull their pieces and edit with editing marks. The next day, hand them back to the students. If you want to talk to the students about something specific, address it in a very short conference first thing. All levels of students can do this as they become comfortable with the process.

Generally, at this point students understand the editing process and use the handout of editing marks to make sense of your editing. If students need pieces edited in the middle of the period, hold the conference then so they can move forward in their writing. These conferences can be held quickly once students understand editing and mostly edit on their own, guided by the editing chart for the marks you make.

The publishing conferences help students make decisions quickly in the publishing process. Section sentences into groups, circle and number them.

Remind the students that this is the text that will go on each page. Once the number of pages is determined, have students determine the size or shape of the book as well as the color of the cover. Pull the number of sheets of paper and construction paper for the book and staple them together. If it is a shape book, pull the pattern and have the student trace it. After doing a few shapes, we found we could make them on the spot during the conference. The shapes should be simple and easy to draw so students have plenty of paper space to write and illustrate (see figures 10.1 and 10.2). Number the pages, reminding the students of the text for each page. Ask where they plan to place the text and illustrations. Remind them of the paratext, such as the cover, title page, dedication, and author's information.

After several weeks, you will find your conferencing rhythm and cadence. Determine what works for you and what doesn't; tweak your conferences so they run smoother and stay within five minutes. You will get better at conferring as time goes by and you become comfortable with the process. You also will find that you enjoy talking to the students about their writing and getting to know them in much deeper ways than before.

MANAGING CONFERENCES

Manage the conferences in ways that work for you so you can see students as quickly as possible with little lag between drafts. Don't let your team or a specialist choose for you; management of your writing conferences is very personal, connected to your personality and style. Choose what works best for you, and don't be afraid to try out your ideas. Teaching and learning go together, and you learn as you go. Over time, it will become simple, second nature, and easily replicated year after year.

Conferences will have movement as you meet face-to-face and one-on-one. Think about your classroom set up, the students, and how you keep order. Several ways to hold conferences are presented here, but they aren't the only ways. Take what you can use, then design your own ways of holding conferences. This is the most important part of writing workshop, because it is differentiated and personal, and it holds the most potential for learning. It takes time for conferring to work just right for you, but don't give up! Continue to work out the kinks as you become more comfortable and confident in your management.

Option 1

The teacher stays at a table, and students come to the teacher. The students line up around the table. Once conferences last less than five minutes, only about two to four students will be there at any time. This way works well with younger students as they have a harder time finding constructive ways of waiting, and their conferences are shorter because they do not write as much. The students who are waiting can either listen to the current conference, gleaning information from it, or whisper read their paper to the next student in line.

Option 2

The teacher stays at the table, and students write their name on the board at the bottom of a list and then return to their desks. They have tasks to do while they wait, such as reread their piece and check it for revisions or edits (whichever conference is upcoming) and put notes or editing marks on their own page. Other ideas for independent work are in the section titled "What Are Students Doing?" The teacher calls students for a conference when it is their turn.

Option 3

The teacher moves around the room with a small chair, crate, or exercise ball in order to sit eye-to-eye with the student. Students write their names on the board when they need a conference and return to their desks, doing tasks while they wait.

Option 4

The teacher moves around the room on a small chair, crate, or exercise ball. Each student has a card on the desk with a different color on each side. If the red side is up, the student is working and doesn't need any help. If the green side is up, the student is ready for a conference. This works for teachers who are good at seeing everything that goes on in the room. The teacher must keep track of who turns a card over and who has the next conference. The downside to this system: if the teacher misses a student, he could wait for a long time. It's best to confer with students in the order in which they are ready for a conference.

At the end of the period a few students will have come into the line or added their name to the list recently. Find out which kind of conference they need and mark it on the Status of the Class sheet for the next day (chapter 18). It reminds you who needs conferences first so you can take them in the order in which they came to you.

We have met teachers who walk around the room and confer at random. The students are expected to have peer conferences or self-conferences at the end of each draft. The problem with this is that students are unaware of the next thing they need to learn because they are not a teacher or the best writer in the class. Writing workshop needs the teacher to move the class and individual students forward in learning the craft of writing. Don't leave learning to chance or to classmates. Conferring in a distinct, reasoned way increases your students' learning. In the conference, check for understanding and push students forward as writers. Only you can do that.

WHAT ARE STUDENTS DOING?

Students' wait for conferences averages five to ten minutes. Because you don't want any downtime in writing workshop, develop independent work for students. The following suggestions need to be taught in a mini-lesson so students are clear about the task. Teach one task at a time and wait a week or more before teaching the next one, allowing students time to gain proficiency at each task. Make an anchor chart listing the ways students can continue to work while waiting for a conference. Add to the chart as you teach mini-lessons on independent activities.

Reading Like a Writer

In reading lessons, the students learn how to *read like a reader*, looking for the main idea, making inferences and drawing conclusions in order to fully comprehend text. In reading like a writer, students read to figure out whether what they are saying will be clear to the reader. At the beginning of their writing experience in your class, having students read their own writing closely and find what they can is enough. Over time, the expectations increase as the skills and knowledge you have explicitly taught in mini-lessons and conferences can be graded and students can be held accountable.

Emphasize how important the skill of reading like a writer is to writers because students will need this skill to do the other independent tasks. Reading one's own work, especially for young writers, can be difficult. Practicing will aid this and help them decide where their paper needs work. If they struggle to read it, so will another reader. Understanding this relationship will help them to be better readers and, of course, better writers.

Asking Questions

Teach the students to question their own pieces. The student reads the whole piece or a paragraph, and then asks questions about whether it answers those questions well. It is hard for a student to look at his own piece this way, but it becomes an important skill when peer conferencing begins. Learning to ask questions and provide feedback to others also increases oral language skills, comprehension, and interpersonal skills.

Finding Nouns

After lessons on nouns and adjectives, have students highlight all of the common nouns, then carefully choose one or more nouns to add adjectives to in order to enhance their meaning.

Checking Conventions

After a mini-lesson on a convention, have students check their papers for that specific convention. Tell them you will try to find mistakes when they come for a conference, so their job is to find all of them before you do. They can circle or underline the mistake, or an area they imagine might be a mistake. Later in the year, they can check for two or more conventions. This motivates them to focus on those conventions and results in shorter editing conferences.

Students can also check spelling by circling words they think are misspelled, then while they wait they can address word walls or the dictionary to find the correct spelling. This is a great way for them pay attention to the phonetic knowledge they have to help them sustain momentum in writing.

Spelling hampers many students, who imagine that spelling a word correctly makes a paper good. They choose simpler words (e.g., "pretty" rather than "gorgeous") merely because they can spell them. Having the power to circle a misspelled word allows students to try new words.

Looking up word spelling can be hard work. When that's the case, making students look up every misspelled word means they only use words they can spell. So help them spell or give them the spelling, depending on the word and its spelling or derivation. You might have a blank word document on the computer where students can spell check single words by typing in the spelling from their paper to see if the word they want is on the spell-check list.

Preparing for Publishing

After publishing several pieces, make publishing materials available so students can access them. They can decide how many pages they want and gather enough paper and the cover for their book. If students already have made several decisions, publishing conferences will go more quickly.

Planning the Illustrations

As an extension of working with picture books, have students plan illustrations for the book. What will be the style? Which medium will they use? Students could sketch a quick storyboard; however, they need to learn about quick sketches so they use the time to plan rather than become engaged in a detailed drawing of one illustration.

All of these suggestions lead well to independent work while waiting for conference. As you go along, you probably will generate more ideas to keep students focused. The key attributes of independent work are that it should be connected to writing, to the students' current pieces, and to reinforcing previously learned concepts. Stay away from meaningless busywork, such as writing spelling words ten times each, looking up definitions, or doing worksheets. These move the students' thinking from writing to other tasks and break up the momentum of working and thinking through the writing process. The focus of independent work should be on writing—specifically, thinking about their current pieces.

Conferences are key to successful writing workshop. Successful conferring focuses on teaching each student what he needs at the time. The students will become better writers and better thinkers about writing through one-on-one interactions tailored to their learning needs.

—⟨ℓ/ℓ/ℓ⟩—

PLANNING JOURNAL: YOUR THOUGHTS ON TEACHER CONFERENCES

Teacher conferences are where most learning occurs, so how you set up conferences and manage them is crucial to the success of writing workshop. Consider several factors as you plan the management of conferences. Plan through the movement of students and materials, and how you will set up the structures students need to grow as writers.

- Where are you located? Where are students located?
- How will you meet with students in order? How will you know which student is next?
- How do the students let you know they need a conference?
- What keeps students working while they wait?
- How will you prepare them for independent work? List mini-lessons needed to prepare them.
- List ways to help you keep conferences under five minutes.

Chapter Fifteen

Peer Conferences

Peer conferences can be powerful, but only at the right time with the right directions. A huge misconception is that peer conferences can take the place of teacher conferences. Students are not teachers. Even your smartest student is still learning the craft of writing. Although students can learn from other students, it is random learning. Students don't have the knowledge, education, training, or ability to teach another student exactly what she needs at that time. Only the teacher can intentionally lead students in the necessary learning to become better writers.

Peers can confer with each other in productive and constructive ways. The goal is to improve the four ways in which students communicate—reading, writing, listening, and speaking—and think about the writing process. Peer conferences can help students learn how to talk about writing in deeper ways. Students can read their own writing, and they can learn to be listeners who then engage the writer in talk about the writing. The focus is on listening to each other and asking good questions that prompt a writer to think about what might be missing or other fundamental craft issues that all fledgling writers have.

A good peer conference follows a procedure, which you will want to model to students during a mini-lesson. A peer conference involves two roles—the reader and the responder—which can be switched after the first conference ends. The reader reads her writing to the peer while the peer listens carefully. Many students do not know how to listen carefully, a skill for another mini-lesson.

Listening carefully involves hearing the story and picturing it. The picture helps the listener notice when the story lacks something. As the responder listens, he forms mental questions about the piece, specifically about what is missing and causing him to question. The responder thinks not only about what is missing but about what is confusing.

When the reader finishes, the responder asks questions about what is missing or confusing, one question at a time. Then he listens to the reader's response. The listener and the reader next discuss how information might be added or rearranged to make it clearer. When reader and responder finish their discussion, the reader may want to jot down a note on the paper to add information for revision.

Peer conferences are only revision conferences. Students are still struggling to understand editing, so they are not ready to edit others' papers in conference. Besides, you still need to edit all students' papers to see where each student is struggling. Editing lets you see class patterns and helps you determine which mini-lessons to teach on conventions.

A peer conference is only an extra conference. You still need a revision conference with each student so you hear him read his story and ask questions that push him to grow in his writing. A peer may ask good questions, but he is only thinking as a reader, whereas you will be listening and responding as a reader and a teacher, thinking about ways to help him become a stronger writer.

Model constructive peer conferences in a mini-lesson. Choose a higher-ability student who speaks clearly and is comfortable in front of an audience, which helps the mini-lesson be clearer and more precise. Choosing a student who is uncomfortable talking in front of the class makes the lesson hard to hear and difficult to understand, which defeats the purpose of the mini-lesson.

Explain how you listen and remind students to look for those signs of listening, such as cocking your head toward the reader and closing your eyes, or looking directly at the reader. The goal is to have students focus solely on what the reader is saying.

Have the student read the piece while you exhibit signs of focused listening. Then question a part you do not understand, listening carefully to the reader's response. Talk about the response; either ask another question or respectfully suggest a revision. The reader responds to the suggestion and decides whether to put a note on his paper. Remind students that the reader can decide whether to take the advice. The responder needs to be OK with that and respect the writer's right to choose his own revisions.

Spend a minute or two explaining your role in the peer conference, and talk about your listening, advising, and reactions to the reader. Students need this metacognitive talk to be effective listeners and responders in a peer conference.

During a peer conference, the writer/reader and the listener/responder practice listening, questioning, responding, and thinking about the craft of writing in deeper ways. They aren't teaching. But they are helping each other in the work civilly and constructively. At the beginning of the teacher conference, question students about their peer conference to gauge how well peer conferences are working.

If you have a break between teacher conferences (yes, it will happen!), listen occasionally to a peer conference, then tweak questioning and discussion in a mini-lesson. Using students' language you hear, help them develop vocabulary to participate in peer conferences. Even if they merely listen to another read, or pay attention to themselves as they read, using peer conferences can increase fluency and impact reading and writing.

Peer conferences are not necessary. You choose whether to engage students in the practice. The younger the student, the more difficult peer conferences are, so it will depend on the age of your students. At the beginning, students are learning the writing process and how to improve their craft. Wait several weeks or months before you throw peer conferences into the mix. You want students to be ready for a new task, especially one as hard as holding peer conferences.

By the time students begin conferring, they should have experienced many conferences with the teacher and be clear on what a conference is. The younger the students, the longer you will want to wait to begin peer conferences. Primary grade students have more on their plate as they are also focusing on forming letters, spelling almost every word, and reading their own writing. This is a lot! Plus, younger students have less experience in academic conversations and need more scaffolding learning how to listen closely and ask questions.

Make an anchor chart as a reminder of the roles and actions of both reader and responder. It is meant to be a resource if students get stuck, so think about what information is necessary, and make it easy to access and read. A two-column, short bulleted list for each person in a peer conference is one style for an anchor chart.

Peer conferences create more noise as students talk quietly about their writing and more movement around the room as they find a place to confer. How you manage the noise and movement partly determines the success of peer conferences. Specific meeting places along the perimeter of the room are usually a good way to ensure less distraction for students who are writing. Students who are ready put their name on the list for a teacher conference, then sit in the peer conference place and wait for another student to do the same. When it is time for a conference, the teacher can interrupt at a stopping place.

Peer conferences have a place in writing workshop, but they do not replace teacher conferences. Peer conferences change the ways in which students talk about writing. When students talk about writing with each other, they learn better self-talk about writing, which leads to better reflection and, thus, better writing.

—⟨ον⟩—

PLANNING JOURNAL: YOUR THOUGHTS ON PEER CONFERENCES

Planning for peer conferences not only involves thinking about what to teach but also about how you manage the extra movement and noise that peer conferences bring. If you decide to have peer conferences, write down what the students need to know and understand about the process, how they will get feedback to become better at it, and where they will position themselves.

- In what area of the room will students meet?
- How will they position themselves, facing each other or side by side?
- How do they keep their place in line for teacher conference?
- How will you teach them to use a quiet voice?
- What mini-lessons do you need to get them started? Which student will help you model a successful peer conference?
- Will you put an anchor chart on the wall to remind them how to conduct peer conferences?
- When will peer conferences begin during the year?

Chapter Sixteen

Student Notebooks

Organizing student work will help students stay organized and keep you organized in a way that maintains your sanity. Students need to find resources, drafts, and finished work easily, reducing the need for teacher help not related directly to writing, thereby freeing you to focus on conferences. Several ways to helping students stay organized are possible. None is the "right" way, so design a way that suits your class and your personality.

ORGANIZING A NOTEBOOK

Students can keep a notebook for organizing notes, handouts, collections, plans, responses, or drafts. It can be a composition or spiral notebook, a file folder, or a binder with tabs. Numerous items can divide a notebook, including tabs, sticky notes, and special folds of pages. Even using two composition notebooks connected with duct tape and divided by duct-tape tabs is possible. Below are some ideas for how to organize the first notebook. Make a section for each subject, or group the items into sections. Sections might (and probably should) include the following:

Topic Collections

Students need a place to write ideas for different pieces of writing. One section in a composition or spiral notebook will keep these lists and ideas together so students can refer to them when they need ideas about what to write about next. Students can add to their collections there when they think of new ideas. Planning the year's mini-lessons on collecting will help determine how many pages to set aside for this section.

Responses

Responding to a mentor text immediately after the mini-lesson in a short burst of writing can be the start to a piece of writing or the jump-start of an idea. These responses can be kept in the same place as topic collections or in a separate section. For these mini-lessons, share a mentor text but without any specific lesson attached. Instead, choose a paragraph or two that includes great descriptive text or talks about a big idea such as friendship, love, care, bullying, othering, or struggling. Just read the passage or text piece, pause a moment, then have students write whatever they want in response to listening to the passage. This helps them make connections between the story and the written word.

Notes

Sometimes students need to take notes on a mini-lesson to use as a reference during their writing process. This greatly depends on the age and ability of the students, as younger students may not be able to write more than a couple of words within the mini-lesson time. Regardless, notes should be short and to the point—usually a bullet list or simple graphic organizer—but notes should never be in sentences. Because mini-lesson time is short, notes act not only as reminders for the students, but also for you to bring up during your conferences with students.

Handouts

Sometimes you give students a handout connected to a mini-lesson rather than having them take notes. This handout should be brief, written on a half sheet of paper to be taped or glued easily into the notebook. Handouts can be different than a note page, maybe including an example text that shows the students how something is done rather than just giving directions.

Handouts can be notes you prepared on a half sheet of paper to be glued into the notebook; they can be complete, or in the form of a chart students fill out during the mini-lesson to help them retain the information. Handouts can be notes ahead that are read and discussed by the students either in pairs, small groups, or whole group. This is a worthy strategy if it is concise information that can be presented in a couple of minutes and you want students to answer a thinking question about when the concept might be used in writing.

Anchor Charts

Sometimes you make large anchor charts to put on the wall as a resource. Having students draw the same anchor chart in their notebooks helps them internalize the concept and is a resource long after the large anchor chart is taken down. You can also copy it on a half sheet of paper for the students to glue or tape in their notebooks. Anchoring their learning with illustrations is a good way to hold students accountable and create autonomy during writing workshop time. Graphic organizers help students think about connections that worded notes or lists cannot.

Personalized Checklists

Having a section of checklists to use before a revision conference or an editing conference will help the students take more initiative revising and editing their own papers. These checklists should be short. You only want to help them focus on their piece for the time it takes you to pull them for the conference they request. Have only five items on a checklist so students can really look for those specific places to revise or edit.

Spelling Lists

Start a list of frequently misspelled words specific to one student and add to it in editing conferences. Instead of correcting the word in the draft, write or have the student write the correct spelling on the list in the notebook. Then he can refer to the list when editing the draft. In addition, the notebook can have a spelling section with notes or handouts on all of the mini-lessons and spelling pattern charts that you have put on the walls. Students can use these as resources long after you have replaced the old word walls with new ones.

Writing Organizers

Planning and organizing for writing pieces can be kept in the notebook or with work in progress. Decide whether you want to see the organizer when you grade the piece. In that case, have students make their organizers on sheets of paper to be kept in the work-in-progress folder (more on this in chapter 19). Otherwise, students can keep all of the organizers in their notebook. One reason to keep them together in a notebook is to view them over time to see how the students are improving in their abilities to organize a topic before writing. That will provide a lot of information about how students learn and use graphic organizers, which can be helpful as you plan your teaching around organizers for future classes.

THE WRITING NOTEBOOK

Don't have students keep their work in progress in the second folder or notebook. It makes it hard for the student to move back and forth between drafts when rewriting. Use file folders to keep work in progress and finished work separate from the resources and lists in the notebook. Keeping work in progress on separate sheets of paper helps students move between two or more drafts or pieces of paper during the writing. If current work in progress is kept together but separate from other pieces, the number of papers is small enough for the students to keep track of and organized each day. Chapter 18 offers more ideas for student organization.

Decide what the students need to put into the notebook before you begin writing workshop. Decide how many blank pages need to be in each section to last students through the year. Students should set up their notebooks on the first day before they begin collecting ideas, label a tab, and then count pages before they place the next tab. Some teachers allow students to decorate their notebooks on the first day.

They can even decorate using things that interest them as a first collection. Or you can decide that notebooks will not be decorated. I have found that reluctant writers spend a lot of class time in the beginning doodling all over their notebooks instead of writing. Once they get into writing workshop, they stop doodling, but those first few weeks are integral to engage students in writing. The more they doodle, the less time they write, which can hinder the reluctant writers' progress—usually they are the slowest writers and the last to become truly engaged in writing workshop.

Notebooks are a good way to keep all the notes, handouts, lists, and mini-anchor charts in one place as a resource, but too often we set them up and forget to use them. Make sure what goes into notebooks are truly resources students can use, and remind them to use them. Before long, even the reminder becomes unnecessary; they go straight to the resource. That is the best way to make the students responsible and resourceful enough to find answers on their own.

—⧸⧸⧸—

PLANNING JOURNAL: YOUR THOUGHTS ON STUDENT NOTEBOOKS

The student notebook can help students stay organized by keeping all notes, handouts, lists, collections, and responses in one place with easy access. Plan how you will have students organize their notebooks and what use the notebooks will have.

- What kind of notebook will you use? Composition or spiral?
- How many sections will there be, and how will they be tabbed?
- What kinds of things will be in each section?
- How many pages will students need in each section for the entire year?
- Where will the students keep the notebooks? Will they keep them in a cubby, their desks, or a filing place all together?

Chapter Seventeen

Collecting Data

Within a week your students will be working in different stages of the writing process, and this will continue for the rest of the year. No two students write at the same speed, and no two pieces will be the same length. When students come for teacher conferences, they may be at the revision stage, the editing stage, or the publishing stage. Writing workshop is very much a teach-as-you-go model based on students' needs at that particular time and guided by the scope and sequence of your school. The big question is: How do you keep up with what the students are doing day to day and over time?

STATUS OF THE CLASS

Status of the Class is a daily record-keeping technique to keep tabs on each student that gives you data for the day and data over time (Atwell, 2014). A simple chart lists students' names down the first column and days of the week across the first row (table 17.1). Right after a mini-lesson and before writing time, announce that it is time for Status of the Class. Call each student's name, and he says what he is working on that day.

Using the writing process, his quick response can be "organizing a topic," "draft 1," "conference for revision," "draft 2," "conference for editing," "draft 3," "conference for publishing," or "publishing." Make abbreviations for each stage, so you can mark the answer quickly. Number the conferences in the order they will happen. This whole process takes no more than a minute or two each day once the students understand how it works and the choices/steps in writing workshop. Then mark on the Status of the Class page throughout the writing time to record conferences or other information. Other abbreviated comments can be added to the little box as well.

Start Status of the Class on the second day of writing workshop, even though everyone will be "organizing." This makes it easier to understand the process of calling a name and getting a quick, no-nonsense answer. On the third day you will get one of two responses, "organizing" and "draft 1," and after that answers will vary for the rest of the year.

At the end of each writing period, write down numbers in the next day's box for each student waiting for a conference, so that none lose their places the next day. You can also number students who come for a conference that day to show all the students who already have been in conference. This quick view of conferences makes sure no one slips through the cracks.

Over time, Status of the Class shows how fast or how slow a student normally works. It shows when students are dawdling, or taking too long on one part of the process. It shows patterns in a student's progress. It works as a safety net, catching students falling through the cracks before it's too late. Table 17.1 shows several patterns (as well as how a chart might look).

You can see that Zachary took four days to publish—too long to spend on one part of the process. With this knowledge, the teacher should have a quick conference with Zachary to ask why he is taking so long and help him speed up his process to become more productive. Zachary also skipped the second draft on his next piece, so either he is rushing or he does not have a complete concept of what revising his piece means. When this happens, a teacher can spot it quickly and move him back to revising.

Zoya is moving quickly through her drafts. Although she is a good writer and is writing above grade-level expectations, the teacher still can challenge her. He should examine her last few pieces to see where she can improve as a writer and make a plan to move her forward in her craft. She may need to develop more complex ways of writing or move to another genre or subgenre to take her writing to the next level.

Alexia took only one day on each draft the first week, but the second week she spent four days on her first draft. A teacher can call her for a conference to talk about the breakdown, then get her going again. Look at the sample Status of the Class in table 17.1 to find other patterns of the students' writing processes.

Keep all of the Status of the Class sheets in a folder, moving current sheets to the back at the end of each week. Then you can pull out several weeks' Status of the Class sheets to check individual students' progress over

Table 17.1. Status of the Class Sample. D1, D2, and D3 are drafts, O is organizing, P is publishing, and C is conference. The superscript numbers are the order in which the conferences were held each day.

	9/16	9/17	9/18	9/19	9/20	9/23	9/24	9/25	9/26	9/27
Sae	D1	D1	D1	D1 C	D2	D2 C^3	D3	D3 C	P	P
Kayla	D2	D2 C	D3 C	P C	P	O	D1	D1 C	D2	D3
Bibesh	P	O	D1	D1	D1 C	D2 C	D3	D3	P C	P
Ian	D2	D2 C	D3	P C	P	P	D1	D1 C	D2 C	D3
Madison	D3	P	O	D1	D2	D3 C	P C^1	D1 C	D2 C	D3
Gianna	D2	D2 C	D3	D3	P C^2	P	P	D1	D1 C^2	D2
Pierre	D1 C^2	D2	D2 C^2	D3	D3 C	P	P	P	D1 C	D2 C
Brianna	P	O	D1 C	D3 C^1	O	D1 C	D2 C	D3 C^1	P C	O
Hamza	D1	D1 C^1	D2	D2 C	D3	P C	P	D1	D1 C	D2
Anh	D1	D1	D1 C^3	D2	D2 C^1	D3	P C	P	P	D1 C
Zoya	D3 C	P	O	D1 C	D2 C	D3 C	P	D1 C^2	D2 C	D3 C^2
Carlos	P	P	D1	D1 C	D2	D2 C^1	D3	P C	P	O
Alexia	D1 C^1	D2 C	D3	P C	P	P	O	D1	D1	D1 C
Sitara	D2 C	D3	P C^1	P	O	D1 C	D2	D2 C	D3 C	P
Sierra	O	D1 C^3	D2	D2	D3	P C^2	P	O	D1	D1 C^1
Zackary	P	P	P	P	O	D1 C	D3	D3	D3 C	P
Justin	D3	P C^2	P	D1	D1 C	D2	D2 C	D3 C	P	O
Brandon	D2	D2	D2 C	D3	D3	P C	P	P	O	D1
Alexandria	O	D1	D1 C	D2	D2	D2 C	D3	D3	D3 C^1	P

time. They show working patterns and breakdowns to address those problems in a timely manner. All of this information keeps students moving along and working smoothly the entire time and gives you direct access to data concerning each student as a writer. Plus, the sheets contain great data for the teaching of writing should your principal or parents like to see how students are progressing and why.

CONFERENCE RECORDS

Although Status of the Class sheets show when you conferred and over what part of the process with each student, it does not show exactly what you talked about. You need to know what specific lessons were taught during conferences because each student is learning something different. A conference record sheet will help you do this; it only need be a piece of lined paper on which you jot down conference notes.

The information you most likely want is the date of the conference, the part of the process that is the conference subject, and what you discussed, written in as few words as possible. Use the same abbreviations as on Status of the Class sheets. Don't get too wordy, or you will take away valuable time from student conferences and run the risk that the line of students waiting for conferences grows.

Here's one way to maintain conference records: keep a notebook or folder with a few pages for each student. Mark these pages with tabs so you can find each student's page easily. When you finish a conference, write your notes and move on.

Another way to keep conference records: place a sheet in each student's work-in-progress folder that stays with the student and can be accessed with his work. That system avoids having another spiral to keep track of but keeps information readily available for evaluations or parent conferences.

Conference records provide information on what you teach each student, so students can be held accountable for their learning. Records help you decide where to move the students in their writing so that they are always growing in their abilities. This is especially helpful to better writers as they write well, which makes it somewhat difficult to know where and when to direct their learning. Conference records also help with parent conferences, giving you specific examples of student learning and progress.

RUBRICS FOR WRITING WORKSHOP

Rubrics can supply a lot of specific data over time. Use them to grade finished pieces, and keep them in the portfolio with the finished pieces. The rubrics and finished pieces together will tell how the student has grown as a writer during the year. Use rubrics designed by your state, district, or grade level, or make your own. See the section on grading (chapter 19) for a rubric that is highly usable due to its autonomy promotion and flexibility.

Status of the Class charts, conference records, and rubrics all help collect the data you need to help students move forward in their writing. The current trend in education focuses on data; this data offers a thorough academic way to talk about the student to administration and parents. It gives a complete picture, both detailed and deep, of each student. It also makes it very easy to keep up with how students are doing in writing workshop, leaving more time to enjoy the process of teaching students to become better writers.

———◦◦◦———

PLANNING JOURNAL: YOUR THOUGHTS ON COLLECTING DATA

Collecting data can help you stay on top of all of the moving pieces of writing workshop. It will remove the fears of what data needs to be collected, either for the school or for you. As you answer the questions, consider how you use the information and whether you need it. Collecting data you don't really use eats up valuable time on unnecessary tasks. Think through these questions and plan how you will collect data. Remember, the district doesn't make data usable. You do.

- What information do you need?
- What will you do with it?
- What information will you collect with Status of the Class?
- What information will you collect about conferences?
- Where will you keep conference sheets?
- Will you use rubrics or another type of record keeping for finished pieces?
- Think about how you can use this information to respond to administration or parents when called upon to discuss why you teach this way.

Chapter Eighteen

Managing Papers

Through all of the drafting and publishing, students must keep papers organized. Helping them be organized helps you be organized, and students who are organized will help you keep track of all of the moving parts of writing workshop. Here are a few tips for organizing the paperwork.

Your Paperwork

You might have mini-lesson plans, Status of the Class charts, conferences sheets, and rubrics. Once you realize that you do not need to make hour-long lesson plans, print class copies of worksheets, or read and grade twenty-five similar papers in one sitting, the paperwork becomes easy to organize. Use a folder or binder for each set of items, or section a spiral notebook for each purpose; that way all the paperwork is in one place and connected. Think about how you will access and use each item so that the organization of those papers will make your work easier.

Status of the Class

Personally, we both like to have these on loose sheets of paper in a folder. That way it is easy to pull out several pages and lay them side by side to look at patterns in students' work and students' progress over several weeks. The page for the current week goes in front; when the week is over, it goes to the back of the stack, so over time the pages are all in order. If that doesn't work for you, try keeping them in a three-ring binder.

Conference Sheets

Conference sheets can be kept in a spiral or a three-ring binder with tabs, or in each student's writing folder and marked right after the conference. This way, students also have a record of the conferences to act as a resource and a reminder for the lessons taught and the individual instruction given during conferences. You may have an idea that works better for you, but make conference records easy to access so you can see conference topics and notes over time.

Rubrics

Rubrics, used to grade finished pieces, give information on how a student is progressing in her writing ability. Keep blank rubrics on a tray or in a folder for easy access. Filled in rubrics for graded pieces can be put in the published piece and kept in a student's portfolio (more on rubrics in chapter 19).

STUDENT PAPERS

A look inside the black hole that is a student's desk shows you how important it is for students to keep their papers organized. Not only will they have easy access, but they won't waste time looking for papers and resources. Students need to keep track of collected topics, organized ideas, resources from mini-lessons, notes, drafts, published pieces, and rubrics. Keep everything organized in the ways that fit best your classroom.

Notebooks and File Folders

Some papers should remain in the notebook, such as collections, organizations, responses to mentor texts, notes, handouts, spelling lists, and mini-anchor charts. These can be stored in the students' desks or cubbies. Students are responsible for keeping track of the notebook and pulling it out as a working resource every day, but you must remind them until using it on a daily basis becomes a habit.

Each student can use a file folder for all drafts of their current piece. Everything is there; students can then use the first draft to write the second draft, the second draft to write the third draft, and so on. When students finish that piece, they turn in the published piece with all of the drafts tucked inside, giving you access to the drafts and notes while you grade.

The students can use a second file folder as a portfolio. When they get back the published piece with a grade, they file it and their rubric in their portfolio. At that time, they can choose to hold onto the drafts or discard them. If you don't let the students take home their published pieces until the end of the year, the growing portfolio is a great way to show administrators and parents students' writing progress.

Keep both of these folders in a hanging file inside a filing cabinet or in a hanging file box or crate on top of a counter or table in the room. Each day students get their folders at the beginning of writing workshop and put them back right before sharing time so they never go inside a desk.

Find a fast, orderly way for students to take and return their folders each day. I usually call students by tables and count to five. Students move quickly, and only a few are at the file box or cabinet at one time. Young children can be a bit impatient, so teach them how to wait for the person in front of them without shoving or pushing. But be sure the folders always go back in the file. Losing a student's work is detrimental to their psyche the next day and can throw off the process for days.

Keeping papers organized so you and the students can access them easily makes the work easier. Without organization, you can get a headache just from all of the moving pieces of writing workshop, but your work is a breeze when everything is organized with a place to store it. Have a system for organizing Status of the Class, conference records, and rubrics and for students to keep their papers organized. Each needs a notebook, a folder with work in progress, and a portfolio. Keeping these in a designated place helps your students learn how to keep their work organized and keeps you sane.

PLANNING JOURNAL: YOUR THOUGHTS ON MANAGING PAPERS

Having a good organization system for your paperwork and the students' paperwork will save time and make writing workshop a smooth operation. Design a system that works for you based on your students, your classroom, and your resources. Answer these questions to help your classroom run smoothly.

- Where will you keep your Status of the Class chart?
- Where will you keep conference records?
- Where will blank rubrics be?
- Where will finished rubrics be?
- Where will students keep their notebooks?
- Where will students keep their drafts for the current piece?
- Where will students turn in finished work?
- Where will students keep their published work? Will they save all of their drafts, or just the published pieces?

Chapter Nineteen

Grading

Most writing teachers give grades on responses to prompts and worksheets connected to conventions, so about now you probably wonder, "How in the world do I grade this?" The answer is simple. It has to do with rubrics and the fact that each student is at a different place in the process.

TRADITIONAL RUBRICS

Traditional rubrics can be used, especially if they are mandated, but they can be too wordy and too narrow to grade a piece of writing quickly and effectively. Consider the rubric in table 19.1, which is a hybrid between a checklist and a rubric. These rubrics are easy to design and have the same objectives as a formal rubric that the state or district mandates. Most important, they are student friendly and attempt to build autonomy for the student.

The goal of a rubric is to show the student what the assignment requires, what he did well or what he missed. In order for a student to understand his writing goals, the rubric needs to be understandable and deliverable. These rubrics allow a student to take ownership of the outcome, knowing that he has met expectations even before he receives a grade.

First, choose what you want to hold the students accountable for and make a list. Then decide how many points to assign to each item. Some formal rubrics use a four-point scale; this can work well when transferring the requirements to the new rubric. You can use a three-point scale for clarity. For instance, a score of 3 means the student did a great job, 2 means the student did an OK job but she has room to improve, 1 means the student tried unsuccessfully, and a score of 0 means the student didn't even try. Vary it so that all of the points end up equaling something that is a divisor of 100. Then just multiply the total points by four or five to get a traditional score for the grade book. Conference sheets, the final paper, and drafts are the data that substantiate your grade.

If students have been faithful to the conferences, revised well, and edited well, then wouldn't all students make a hundred every time? This is where professional judgment comes in.

Grades are meant to show parents and administrators how well the students grasp concepts at the grade level. If a student is working on grade level and works hard, then the student should make a good grade. If a student is working below grade level, then it is important to show that through the grade. Use the comments section to explain why a student has not made a 3, based on the expectations of the grade level.

Suppose the class has been working on commas, and a student working below grade level has only one sentence with a comma because she does not have any compound or complex sentences. Then give a 1 or 2 with an explanation that the skill is not being used enough. As a professional, you know the grade-level expectations, where each student is working, and where each is capable of working. Your professional judgment is valuable and sound; how you talk about the work is important in helping students grow as learners and writers.

These rubrics are easy for students to understand. Giving students formal rubrics and going over them in class makes the teacher feel as if the student was told what was expected. However, using the Wilson and Puente (2014) style rubric, shown in table 19.1, children not only are told what is needed, but can be held accountable because it is clear, readable, and the list is age and skill friendly. With this new kind of rubric, a student can use it as a resource to double-check what he will be held accountable for, even as he waits for a teacher conference. When a student questions what is required, have him check the rubric; it is easy enough to understand and usually answers the question. It helps students become more autonomous.

Using this rubric lets the teacher give points for quality and explain why she gave those points. It gives the student more information about the grade he earned and where he might improve on his next piece of writing. But most of all, the rubric connects the grade to the work.

Table 19.1.   Writing Rubric (Wilson, 2015).

Objective	Grade	Explanation (if needed)
The beginning connects to the reader.	2	
The main idea is clearly stated in the introduction.	3	
The body has details that make things clear.	3	
The main idea is clearly stated in the ending.	3	
The ending connects back to the reader and to the world.	3	
All sentences begin with a capital.	3	
All sentences end with a period.	3	
Total	20	

MANAGING THE GRADING

It may seem hard to keep up with grades as students finish at different times, and some students finish fewer pieces because they work slower. Because students are staggered in their work, only one or two students publish each day. You can grade those one or two published pieces in five minutes after school. By this time, you know the piece: you've walked with the student through the drafts and seen the transformation. Just remind yourself what the student did during the process and quickly check the published piece to fill in the rubric.

Usually teachers are required to give a certain number of grades each week in each subject. You may be told to give a composition grade and a convention grade each week. This is handled easily: separate the rubric into these two parts and give a score for each section. Most students are able to complete one published piece in about a week, but what about slower writers? You can handle this issue two ways. You can look at the unfinished work's progress at week's end and give a score for what the child has accomplished, or double the score she gets when she does finish.

Two things make grading in writing workshop easy: First, the redone rubric is easy to use and make comments and easy for the student to use and understand. Second, the rubric gives you, parents, and administrators detailed information about each student's work. The absolutely best thing about grading in writing workshop? You never have to read twenty of the same papers again, because each piece is authentic and different.

—⟨⟩—

PLANNING JOURNAL: YOUR THOUGHTS ON GRADING

Develop your first rubric. If you like the one in table 19.1, just tweak it to fit your class. Change it throughout the year depending on what genre or standards the students' work is focused. As the students grow in their writing ability, your rubrics change to assess the growth. Here are some questions you need to answer.

- How many grades do I need each week?
- Must they be specific to content?
- What will I do for those students who take two weeks to finish a piece?
- When will I teach a mini-lesson on the rubric?
- How will I change the rubric as genres change or new concepts are learned?
- Will I follow the traditional rubric closely in my new rubric, so when asked if I'm using the formal one, I can answer "yes"?

Chapter Twenty

A Schedule for the First Ten Days

Getting started is the most difficult thing about writing workshop. Students have a great deal to grasp so that the workshop continues over time with clear instruction, knowledge, and increasing autonomy. It is hard for the teacher as well; she must attend to all of the things her students are working to learn as well. Think about what they need to know on the first day to get started, and then the second. Take it one step at a time. Ease everyone into the process. Over time it gets easier, and the work gets better.

The students only need to understand a few things on the first day. They need to know the structure of writing workshop and that it will happen every day with the same schedule. They need an overview of the writing process, but they don't need to know it deeply at this time. They students only need to have an idea where they are headed. They will gain a more complete picture of the writing process after they complete their first piece.

The students need to know the organization of the classroom, what each folder and the notebook is for in order to put everything in its place at the end of the period. Knowing the purpose of the notebooks and organizing them will be part of that teaching. Finally, students need to begin collecting topics. That is a lot for the first day. The schedule will be a little skewed, including several mini-lessons for introductions and procedures, a short time for collecting, and a short time for informal sharing with a peer.

From that day on, introduce each part of writing workshop more in-depth, modeling how to work through the process. This is when the mentor text that you wrote in part I becomes important. Each day the mini-lesson's goal is to teach the next step in the process. Use your text as a mentor text as you model thinking, writing, revising, conferring, rewriting, editing, publishing, and sharing.

Once you have gone all the way through the process in the mini-lessons for the first two weeks, move on to specific aspects of being a good writer, using other mentor texts and anchor charts as you settle in to the routine of writing workshop. Be careful: you can get caught up in the love of the lesson and lose track of time. Although beginning lessons take more time, remember to get students writing quickly. In early grades, this lesson can be as simple has how to hold a pencil or paper correctly or how to write their name. For the upper grades, get on with it. They're ready to begin a new type of writing that is for them, about them, and with them.

This schedule outlines the mini-lesson and sharing time for each day. Give students the bulk of the time to write (except on the first day).

Day 1. Mini-lessons on writing workshop and the structure, the writing process overview, the procedures for materials, setting up the notebook, and collecting. Students set up their notebooks and create their first collection of topics. Have pairs of students share their topics with each other.

Day 2. Model choosing a topic and organizing what you will write about. During writing, move around the classroom and have students tell you about their organizers. Have them share interesting topics from the day before.

Day 3. Model using your organizer to write the first draft, writing in front of the students. Show students the procedures for conferences. Have students share their organizers with each other. The students' work will begin to stagger, with some students still working on their organizers and some writing first drafts. Have your first revision conferences.

Day 4. Model having a revision conference with yourself, using your completed first draft. For sharing today, have students share their first drafts in pairs.

Day 5. Model revising and rewriting your piece. For share time, choose a student to share with the class what he is working on.

Day 6. Introduce editing marks and have students put the chart in their notebooks. Model having an editing conference. Choose a student to share with the class what she is working on.

Day 7. Model editing and rewriting your piece. Choose a student to share with the class what he is working on.

Day 8. Model having a publishing conference with yourself. One student probably has finished the whole process by this time. From that point on, share the students' finished work during share time.

Day 9. Model writing and illustrating your published piece.

Day 10. Model sharing by sharing your finished piece. Also model how an audience should act.

This plan for the first ten days gives students solid ground to write on as they move through the writing process piece after piece. After ten days, you begin to decide what to teach in mini-lessons based on students' needs, the school or district time line, and the standards. Set a schedule to work on conventions on certain days of the week and begin to show other mentor texts to highlight good writing. Remember, come back to your own writing as a mentor text periodically throughout the year as you are the best writer in the class.

Chapter Twenty-One

Writer Development by Grade

EMERGING WRITERS: KINDERGARTEN

Writing is communication in written form, and it begins with pictures. Before young children know letters or sounds, they know how to tell their stories. If children want to tell their stories on paper, they use drawings. This is where writing begins.

Writing workshop is an authentic form for teaching students how to write well. Kindergarteners can do writing workshop, but it may look very different as they are just learning letters, sounds, and words. If you teach kindergarten or first grade, the steps of the writing process will stay the same, but the content will be very different as students move from pictures to letters to words to sentences.

Think about the development of writing. The first phase is telling stories verbally and drawing pictures of their stories. Students come to school with varying commands of spoken English. Whatever their skill level, begin there and build on these skills during the year. Pictures are humans' first writing. Within a simple drawing of a stick figure—just a head, legs, and arms holding an object—is a story about a person doing something.

In the second phase, the child begins making random letters to tell a story about the letters even if they don't correspond to the sounds in the words used to tell the story. The child is learning that letters are always part of a story and go with the pictures.

Next, the child writes the first letters of each word, stringing them together to make a sentence. He begins to learn that the letters have sounds, and the first sounds of every word are the sounds he notices first. After this the letters slowly turn into phonetically spelled words.

Finally, each student moves slowly to correct spellings of high-frequency words until he has a good mixture of correctly and phonetically spelled words as he gains confidence in writing out his stories.

These are the phases of emergent writing, and moving students through these phases and into completely written pieces is the goal. But every student is different. Each comes from a different family with different exposure to text and different abilities. Therefore, students move through the phases at different speeds, but all in that particular order.

Some kindergarteners write stories with words; some students will not reach that point until sometime in first grade. If you teach at the kindergarten or first-grade level, your goal for writing workshop is to find out where a student is, encourage her movement through that stage, and know where she needs to move next. Writing workshop, even in the lower grades, allows a teacher to see growth and variability, and build strength over time.

Storytelling

Young children have stories. Sometimes the stories reflect something that happened to them, and sometimes the stories are ones they make up in their play. They collect their stories by telling them to you and their peers on a regular basis. Have them choose a partner and tell a story. After each student has a turn, have students draw a picture of the story. For sharing, pick two or three students to share their pictures.

Revision Conference and Rewrites

The pictures that students collect can either be their first draft or it can be the idea for the first draft. Either way, this will be the time to have revision conferences with the students.

Your part still is to figure out what the piece needs most and what will help the writer grow.

Start the conference by having the student tell you about the picture. Then ask questions about the picture, understanding that it is the story. Are parts missing parts from the picture? Are parts there that don't belong because they are not part of the story? Talk to the student about what to change in the picture. Then, have her draw another picture with the changes. At this point have the student think about what the caption will say, and encourage her to try to write it, depending on her current letter/sound skills.

It may be difficult for students to grasp the idea of redrawing the same picture again but with slight differences. Model doing this with a picture you draw; you may have to model this revision stage several days in a row.

During the revision process, each young student draws the same picture with the changes you talked about in the conference and writes a caption for the picture. It doesn't matter whether letters are random or even scribbles the student calls writing. Each is trying out writing in the way he knows, and you will move him forward in his learning. As he better understands how written language works, he begins to write more and more.

Editing, Conferring, Drafting, and Publishing

Now talk with each student about his picture and have him read the caption to you. Then write it for him, thinking out loud and explaining what sounds the letters make, how to form letters, how to leave space between words, and why we put periods at the end of sentences.

Then have students redraw the pictures, making them especially nice, and write the captions. The edited draft and publishing can be together at this point because the illustration already is part of this draft, and the students will be doing their best work. Again, you may have to model this several times in a row so students understands that they are drawing the same picture with small changes to make it look its best. This may be the first time students experience redoing work to improve it.

Structure of Writing Workshop for Early Grades

Kindergarten students are learning how to do school: standing in line, taking turns, following directions. Structuring whole-class writing workshop might be a bit like herding cats; restructure it and incorporate it into a rotation for centers. Still, start with a mini-lesson on writing. It can be as described in chapter 14, or it can be shared writing as it connects to the overall flow in writing. Conferring can be one center; writing, another. The other two centers could be some other kind of literacy learning. In the writing center, students work on their pieces no matter where they are in the process.

At the conference center, confer with students in that group. Conferences will be short because the pieces are short. When you confer with one student, the others in the group can watch and learn, too, or they can continue to work on their own writing. This way you can meet with every student every day.

Sharing can be the same as it is with older children; however, more children will publish each day. It won't take long to read each piece, so three or four children can share in the five- to ten-minute time frame.

As the students' writing evolves, so can the structure of writing workshop. The nonnegotiables are these: a mini-lesson, writing time, conference time, and sharing time every day. Use your creativity and professional knowledge to structure and move around those processes.

BLOSSOMING INTO WRITERS: FIRST GRADE

As the students move into first grade, the picture still is the most important part of their story, but the text plays a growing role in their stories as they move forward. Picture and text interact to make the full story. Your goal is to move them to a place where only text is used in the drafting process, and pictures become illustrations in the publishing phase.

Organizing and the First Draft

At the beginning of the year, the picture is how the students organize their thoughts. Have students also write a sentence to go with the picture. This is their first draft. Some students will want to write more; definitely encourage that. But the lowest expectation at this point is to write one sentence.

As the year progresses, expect students to write a more complete story with several sentences. Around January begin modeling simple graphic organizers with key words, and by the end of the year, expect all students to use only text for the first draft.

Paper that is half blank and half lines works well with kindergarteners and first graders. As first grade progresses, the lines for writing should become smaller and smaller, leading to the next step—using notebook paper.

Revising, Editing, and Publishing

Because many of the students will have a sentence rather than a story, in the revision conference talk about aiming to write three sentences: a beginning, a middle, and an end. Sequencing is a major thing students learn about stories at this age. Talk about what happens first, second, and last. As they tell you, write a key word for each section with a number beside it so they can remember the order when they begin to rewrite.

Editing is done much the same as the upper grades, except the focus for most of the year is mainly on capitals, periods, and spelling. Word walls or handouts for the notebook listing high-frequency words will come in very handy.

At first, publishing can be a polished picture with correct, nicely printed text at the bottom of the page. As students move from picture drafting into drafting with only text, introduce books as a means of publishing to excite and encourage them to move into text drafting.

Kindergarten and first grade can be a fun time in learning to write because you see so much growth. Students go from knowing hardly anything about text to reading and writing full sentences, which comes naturally if given the chance to grow at their own pace. Writing workshop allows them the freedom to grow naturally as writers, moving through the emergent stages into communicating with text in complete sentences.

WE ARE WRITERS: SECOND AND THIRD GRADES

As children emerge from learning to read and write in first grade, they begin to build and fine-tune their literacy skills. Most second graders are able to write sentences, having stronger skills in writing letters and words. Because they are becoming experts at decoding, they are able to spell and, thus, share what they think. At that point they are ready to learn how to write sentences clearly to tell a story by sequencing multiple events. In doing this, they become increasingly aware of extraneous information that often accompanies young people's oral storytelling but is not appropriate for written text.

Development as Writers

As second graders move into third grade, they continue to strengthen their writing; pieces become longer, and students move from a more orally based story to a written one. The growth will be exponential and easy to spot. When a young person begins to refigure how oral language becomes written language in real ways, he begins to write prolifically. It is the opening of the talk no adult wants to listen to. Writing becomes the means of sharing all that is important to younger students.

Illustrations are left solely for the publishing phase, meaning that for writers, illustrations are not the writing of the story or piece as they were for the younger grades. Instead, they become art that enhances the writing. The art of illustration must be taught to students so that it isn't about "drawing a picture" but about showcasing their thinking in powerful ways that enhance their writing.

At the beginning of the year, most second- and third-grade students write four to six sentences. Some, of course, write more, and some begin with only one sentence. Accept what each student produces and believe that it is what he has to offer at this point. Then, during the first revision conference, talk about what he can add to the story. If the student has only written one sentence, encourage him to add two more sentences. This will set up the piece for a beginning, middle, and end sequence that will help the student structure his pieces correctly from the start.

Notice that you facilitate the next step. This is what makes writing workshop so important for the growth of each student: it is tailored to the needs of the individual. It naturally differentiates at the crucial times that she needs it. So, your writer of few words needs to be pushed to tell the entire story. A writer who moves from place to place without a plot needs to know what a plot is and why a central theme is important. Cater your mini-lessons as well as your conferences. As you help writers to see how to make their writing better right then, you increase their efficacy as writers as well as your own efficacy to help each child in your class.

Spelling

The students' goal is to write well, and they naturally equate writing well with spelling words correctly. It is developmental. Because spelling has been a focus during their years learning phonics and engaging in spelling and vocabulary lists, it is natural for them to think that spelling correctly is the goal. Think about how much time has been spent in their young years learning about the sound system, spelling patterns, and other scientifically based reading methods. These methods have served them well, and they are the reason beginning writers can make words into meaningful sentences.

At second and third grades, almost all students ask for the spellings of words. In every classroom teachers hear, "How do you spell. . . ." If you give in and spell words for them, they do not autonomously use their knowledge about spelling. At the same time, you can set them up to be more independent and have a better work ethic. Make figuring out spellings prominent in mini-lessons; give students myriad strategies to use the spelling science they learn in guided reading and language arts experience.

Remember, "sound it out" works about 75 percent of the time. Although the other 25 percent seemingly is a lot, it is important that students use the strategies they know. At the same time, have them spell words the way they sound in the first draft to keep their writing going so they can sustain the momentum. The story is the most important part of the first draft because the ideas percolating in the student's head are being put on paper. If a writer gets stuck on a word because it "needs to be correct," it stops the flow and disrupts his concentration. Handle this early or it will hinder the writing process for these novices.

Structure and Genres

One goal at this age is to get students to write lengthier pieces. Another goal is get them to structure their pieces more coherently, focusing on the content and presentation of the piece rather than writing for an audience or solely for the teacher's approval. Although the length and the cohesiveness of the piece are two different aspects of writing, work on one can improve the other.

As students write longer pieces, they simultaneously add more details and aid the reader's comprehension as the story becomes more coherent. Having students work on making their story easy to read and understand often lengthens the story. The longer and more structurally sound the piece, the better it reads. For early writers, often the writer struggles with reading his own piece because he has left out information. These details enable the reader (who is the writer) to communicate his ideas for others to understand and enjoy.

The students can use these two years to learn about genres of writing. Whereas kindergarten and first-grade students mostly write personal narrative, second and third graders can experiment with poetry, nonfiction, expository, and persuasive pieces. They still write more personal narrative and memoir as they hone their writing skills because as early writers, they fuse their writing with the egocentric world around them by telling about themselves and their experience. Learning about and experimenting with other genres will help older, somewhat more experienced writers branch out.

Set up the year so that students can learn about different genres through mini-lessons and mentor texts. Require them to write one piece in a different genre once every six to nine weeks; that gives them the experience they need in different modes of writing. Experience is the name of the game in writing.

No matter what age, novice writers need experience. No poet or speechwriter writes the best the first time he tries the genre. Each student needs specialized attention and practice within the genre, so when he encounters issues he can rectify them as he becomes more fluent.

Expectations and Instructional Levels

Although second and third graders have been telling, listening to, and reading stories for several years, they have less experience with poetry and informational texts. Making sure they are exposed to other genres during reading, and read alouds help them to work through problems in writing their own pieces in different genres.

Adjust your expectations to the children's instructional level. Remember, they need the freedom to try new things without worrying about perfection. Don't fall into the trap of deficit thinking, measuring all students against an overly high bar. These writers have been writing for only a couple of years and have not mastered it yet. Make sure parents are aware that they might see writing that has not been corrected to perfection. But expect students to show facility with the writing process, growing over time.

To see this growth, you can't judge from one piece of writing. Compare papers over time; see that skills are improving throughout the year. However, if you taught a skill and worked on it with students, hold them accountable for it. Don't be afraid to enforce a skill you have taught; just make sure students understand it and know how to use it.

Students at this stage tend to focus on the events in the sequence of their story. Gently nudge them toward commenting on their emotions and thoughts during the story event, making meaning from their experience and giving the pieces that "so what?" emphasis. It can include their senses, which enable more description that includes what they see, hear, smell, taste, and touch. But don't stop there. Keep nudging them to think about the core issues in their pieces As they think more about their emotions and the significance of them, students connect them to their humanness and, more important, to the shared humanness of the reader. It makes the stories better and enables connection between the writer/reader and the audience.

Sometime in the third grade, almost all students discover and can be taught about paragraphs. Paragraphs are a hard concept developmentally because even facile writers sometimes wonder whether they need a paragraph, or attempt to make a paragraph every four or five sentences because it "seems about right."

Kathy once looped a class from second to third to fourth grade, which gave her a special ability to see the developmental and taught growth of those students. For example, indention was always a second-grade standard, but try as she might, she never felt successful in teaching her students to indent paragraphs. Mainly, the students were not really writing paragraphs in second grade. Those who needed paragraphs struggled to know when or how, and would make comments such as, "I'll just put one here." Often she let the skill go, thinking someone would teach it in third grade. But, because she looped with her class to third grade, what happened surprised her.

When students naturally began writing longer pieces, she found that they felt a need to separate the writing into smaller chunks and began to skip lines where the topic changed a little. When this happened, Kathy used it as a teachable moment and talked in conference about paragraphs and indenting. When several children exhibited the same writing behavior, it was time to reteach paragraphs to the class in a mini-lesson. Usually, in the next draft or the next piece students automatically began paragraphing. Sometimes they were right about where a paragraph should go, sometimes a little off, but all recognized that they needed paragraphs in their increasing long story. This is an example of students who were ready for the concept of paragraphs and felt a need for it in their writing, and so they learned it and applied it to all of their writing.

Each standard in English/language arts will have more than is appropriate for the writers you are working with. Look at standards in kindergarten; they will be similar to those of the first and second grades. So will standards for fourth and fifth grades. Each might have a bit more depth, but the standard remains the same. They often begin, "Students will use correct conventions." This standard will be the same for kindergarten through fourth. As a teacher, you know that in kindergarten little will be done with conventions other than a period when a student has written a sentence using phonetic and discovery spelling. The expectation will be different than that of a fourth grader. Teachers must be even more conscious of this because learners are all different and fit within the development of English/language arts skills a bit differently as well; some are faster and some slower.

Second and third grades are a joy to teach writing because students still have a child's view of the world in all of its wonder but enough literacy skills to write about their point of view in detail. Remembering that they are in a constant state of growth and are cognizant of what writing a good piece sounds like will help you continually move them forward.

A WRITER IS WHO I AM: FOURTH AND FIFTH GRADES

Sometime during the fourth and fifth grades, children begin to ponder the world outside their own experiences and perspectives and want to share their ideas. Many begin to think abstractly, viewing the world not just in the concrete, physical world of childhood, but also in the ethereal world of possibilities of life on Earth. They begin to read fantasy and science fiction books as well as developing a taste for nonfiction topics. During this time, dragons and fairies, hippopotamuses, and space travel become real possibilities, dreams they want to discuss through their writing. They also begin to ask the question "Who am I?" Ideas such as these can help design writing workshop to propel them forward in their writing. Listening and using instruction are easier for fledgling writers if the teacher uses examples students are interested in.

Remember, your students have heard about the basic conventions before. In previous school experience they were exposed to nouns, verbs, adjectives, prepositions, periods, question marks, exclamation marks, commas, and semicolons. Even if you imagine that the teacher before "did nothing" to prepare them, most did. The teaching profession is filled with good teachers who, like you, need to make choices. They focused on a knowledge or skill that enabled a child who was not previously using it to do so. You just might not be privy to the work that teacher did.

So students in fourth and fifth grade do not need more lessons on the basic use of these conventions; rather, they need instruction and practice in using these conventions with finesse, creating ever more complex sentences to explain their experiences and points of view to the world. They can move forward in their thinking and sentence construction in ways that will surprise you.

You will be tempted to provide worksheets or other modes of practice of a particular skill as high-stakes tests often have a section for these seemingly discrete skills. Be wary. If they can do it in their own writing, they can do it as a skill on a test, but not the other way around. Just because a student can fix an issue with a sentence on a worksheet doesn't mean he can in his own writing. How many of us have taught a skill, seen the student complete the skill correctly on a worksheet, then seen him not do it in his own writing or on a six-week test? Skills must be usable in students' own writing to be transferrable.

The key to what to teach comes from the students as they read different genres and notice differences in those writings. Those differences will propel them to want to use these new ways in their writing. When conferring with fourth and fifth graders, notice what they naturally do and experiment with, then talk about and show them how to do it effectively in their own writing. This makes teaching conventions a breeze.

Every child gets what she needs when she needs it to move forward through the conferences because each conference is geared to her and her writing. This is powerful for you and the student. The student should feel that the conference helped her writing in the way *she* thinks it should be better (she has more experience now and will not just focus on conventions) and the ways *you* think it should be better (don't just focus on conventions either if you want writing to become better, as writing scores reflect that teaching).

Quality, Not Quantity

Students' writing naturally gets longer at this point; but the goal is to write better, not more. Help students write pieces one or two pages long but much more powerful. They will grow as writers and make grading and conferences more manageable. Students who equate writing with length have begun to imagine that the best writing they read is long. Chapter books and movies they see reinforce this. So make sure explicitly to showcase good writing that is shorter. Speak powerfully about this, and be sure to show pieces that meet this need. You don't want writers who are writing just to have length. Comments such as, "Mine is five pages" and "Well, mine is seven" are clues that this is happening.

Don't squelch students' initial excitement as they show they love writing. If you notice several subjects in one piece, help them focus on just one subject. Maybe a student vacationed in three different states; have him write about only one. If he wants to write about all of them, he can write three different pieces, or a chapter book in which each chapter becomes a piece for revising, editing, and grading. Remember, be explicit that you aren't cutting or deleting the text, but that he has too much text for one piece and the other text can be used to make a new story! Promote this concept; it leads to exciting discussion.

Seeing lines drawn through text can be disheartening to a burgeoning writer, so do it carefully. Ensure that you are super excited about the possibilities the part you crossed out can bring to a different piece, even use a colored highlighter or underline it in a purple pen to show that the part might not fit in this piece, but that it might in another. Teach a mini-lesson about using parts from previous pieces. The highlighting or underlining will help students look back and see the parts they might use again.

The most interesting aspect of teaching fourth and fifth graders writing is getting them to think about the deeper meaning behind each piece. They are ready to think about bigger ideas and attach those ideas to events in their lives. They want others to know that they have personal lives with their inherent complications and issues even though they are not adults. Push students to center their pieces around a "so what?" point, moving them from just writing about a day in their lives to a day that changed their viewpoint on life. Teach students about theses and push them toward a main idea; it will bring cohesion to their writing, raising it far beyond your expectations and previous experience and, more important, beyond theirs. Once a student sees himself as a writer, good, plentiful writing follows.

Genres

Poetry

The "so what?" push propels them during poetry writing, too. Descriptions and emotions are at the center of writing poetry, and every young tween has those. But the point of a poem is to have the listener or reader think deeply about the embedded ideas. Encourage students to explore and experiment with poetry, playing with language and images and emotions. Whether they use rhyme or write free verse is not important; learning how to convey imagery, use metaphors, and bring forth emotions is the goal of writing poetry.

Poetry is very personal, making it a great genre to get the students to think about their own values and perceptions as they work to make sense of their world. Using fewer words more powerfully can help students share emotions for themselves and for others. Slam poetry and lyrical rhyme are newer ways poetry is being used to convey deep meaning. Explore some of this with your youngsters; they listen to it and find meaning in it. Given some freedom of expression, they will surprise and impress you with their knowledge of verse and rhyme within such songs.

Nonfiction and Informational Texts

Fourth and fifth graders are moving outside their home–school world and noticing the bigger environment and issues inherent in that world. They begin to realize places beyond their neighborhood have different ideas and customs, different people with different lived experiences. Writing nonfiction or informational texts give students a reason to study topics of interest and write about what they learned. In research writing, students read and learn, then compose information into a new piece. The research involves reading, note-taking, organizing, and composing. Don't think of the note cards of old; instead, think about new topics and technology that is faster and newer than the researched spaces of many of our past experiences. Take steps to help children enjoy the genre they are increasingly drawn to as they discover new things about their world and the things in it.

The first step in teaching students to write informational text is to read about the topic, searching for information to use in their pieces. Many students want to skip this step, but it is the most important step in writing a piece that is knowledgeable, using correct facts and ideas. Students need to read to learn and understand, and then reread as they take notes. The first reading helps the student move to a focus for his topic. The rereading helps him decide what information he needs to put in his notes. Rereading not only helps reading fluency and comprehension, but it helps him decide what to add to the piece. Nonfiction books include much extraneous and scientific information. Only as students become "expert" in an area can they begin to add such facts to their writing and, thus, their thinking.

Taking notes is the next step. Students want to just copy information from a book or website, usually whole sentences verbatim. Students need instruction on how to take notes. The reread makes it easier for them to pick out facts and write them in figures, abbreviations, single words, and/or short phrases. These notes become the organizer or document that helps students organize their writing. They can color code notes based on subtopics, and these subtopics can be the paragraphs for an essay or informational piece. Or they might keep different pages for different topics they are writing about— one page about foods a rhino eats and rhino habitat, another about poaching, and a third about drones that are helping the rhino population. Obviously, many topics that can be included, and most children will not include them all. However, their goal is to become more expert than their peers and be able to write and talk about their topic in real, substantial ways.

Although they might have experimented with essays in third grade, fourth and fifth graders are ready to try out new ways of becoming writers and gain experience with the form and format of an essay. However, the more essays they write, the better they will become, so assign essays in other subjects such as reading, science, or social studies. They can use the skills they have learned in writing workshop to put together essays in subject areas where you can assign similar readings and have them take a stand and form an opinion about the topic of study.

In reading, students can evaluate a character's actions, making points from the text. In social studies, students can draw conclusions about historical events. In science, students can compare and contrast scientific concepts. Because in writing workshop they think about and use their writing in novel ways with direct, differentiated feedback, they are more facile when using it in new subject areas.

Often kids are unlikely to use something they learned in science in reading because they departmentalize their learning, as you do in lesson plans. It has been done this way for years, but it is not a good way for kids to cross-pollinate their knowledge and skills. So, think about ways to cross into other subject areas, including talking to teachers in other areas (if you are departmentalized, which is common in fourth and fifth grades) and ensuring that your area is writing in real ways. It matters not what subject you teach; writing substantiates learning and adds to students' reading comprehension.

Older students are ready to fly in their writing in fourth and fifth grade. Often they cannot write as fast as their brains think. If you have reluctant young writers, it is because they have not been able to choose their topics, feel uncomfortable sharing their thoughts, or, characteristically, are scared to be wrong. You must help this by having fun with the students as they explore, revise, and learn about their world through writing. It will happen.

Conclusion

Being able to communicate by speaking, listening, reading, and writing makes us human. From the time we enter school, we work with trained professionals to learn how to read and write in order to communicate our thoughts, experiences, and hopes both for ourselves and for those who come after us with increasing aptitude. Writing workshop helps students with all of these forms of communication. It is authentic and personal and is the best way to teach writers how to compose because it teaches the writer, not a subject.

It is differentiated instruction at its best, as it is one-on-one instruction using students' own works and thoughts. Students learn how to write well through writing workshop no matter their age, intellectual ability, socioeconomic status, ethnicity, culture, first language, or dialect. It works for everyone because it is tailored to each individual's needs. It draws learners in and engages them in deep and complex thinking.

People young or old are motivated by writing workshop because they write about subjects that interest them and express themselves in unique ways. They become better problem-solvers as they struggle through the complexity of their own writing in order to say exactly what they want. Students enjoy writing because it gives them agency in a world where young people have little agency.

As humans, we think deeply as we write, shifting words and sentences to find our voice. Imagine how it would feel to have a knowledgeable adult meet your needs as you navigated that path, providing you with a workshop as you tell the world who you are and why you have value. That is what writing workshop does for even the youngest in our schools. It gives each person differentiated help and personal value.

With writing workshop, you get to be the kind of teacher you want to be, not one worried about a worksheet not being done but one who knows the development of your students, one who uses data to discuss the reading and writing needs of each student. As you move through each piece of writing with your students, you will get to know them on a deep and personal level. You will learn about them as thinkers, workers, writers, and human beings. More important, students will learn about themselves and who they are in their families, their classrooms, and the world. This is what teaching is all about—learning.

References

Atwell, N. (2014). *In the middle: A lifetime of learning about writing, reading,a nd adolescents*. Portsmouth, NH: Heinemann.

Babbitt, N. (1975). *Tuck everlasting*. New York: Farrar, Straus and Giroux.

Barnett, Mac. (2012). *Extra yarn*. New York: Balzer + Bray.

Cisneros, S. (1991). *The house on Mango Street*. New York: Vintage Books.

Cleary, B. (1999). *A mink, a fink, a skating rink: What is a noun?* Minneapolis, MN: Carolrhoda Books.

Gallagher, K. (2011). *Write like this: Teaching real-world writing through modeling & mentor texts*. Portland, ME: Stenhouse.

Godley, A. J., Carpenter, B. D., & Werner, C. A. (2007). "I'll speak in proper slang": Language ideologies in a daily editing activity. *Reading Research Quarterly, 42*(1) 100–131.

Heard, G. (2016). *Heart maps: Helping students create and craft authentic writing*. Portsmouth, NH: Heinemann.

Henkes, K. (1996). *Lilly's purple plastic purse*. New York: Greenwillow Books.

Hutchins, P. (1968). *Rosie's walk*. New York: Simon & Schuster.

Weaver, C., Bush, J., Anderson, J., & Bills, P. (2006). Grammar intertwined throughout the writing process: An "inch wide and a mile deep." *English Teaching: Practice and Critique, 5*(1) 77–101.

Wilson, J. C., & Puente, K. (2014, January). "Rubrics: The long and short of it." Paper presented at Hawaii International Conference on Education. Honolulu, HI.

About the Authors

Kathleen Puente has been an educator for more than thirty years, beginning as a special education assistant. She received a bachelor's in elementary education and a master's in literacy education from the University of Texas at San Antonio. She has taught grades 1–4 in the regular classroom setting and grades K–5 as a gifted and talented specialist. She has taught writing workshop to numerous groups throughout the years and has been a presenter with the San Antonio Writing Project. She is currently an adjunct at Education Service Center 20, working with in-service teachers in English language arts and gifted education, and an adjunct professor at Texas A&M University, San Antonio, working with student teachers as they prepare for their careers in education.

From her first year of teaching second grade, Kathy has engaged her students in writing workshop. Over the years, she has gained experience and grown with her students in writing and life as they have become engaged in the joys of writing as an expression of who they are. She has seen the phenomenal growth that writing workshop brings to students as they move through the process again and again, finding joy not only in writing, but also joy in life.

She travels to Liberia, West Africa, where she works with teachers in nine schools in Brewerville, Massaquoi, and Kokoyah on reading and writing instruction. She has collected more than forty thousand books in the United States and shipped them to Liberia, where she helped schools set up working libraries and trained new librarians and teachers in using the books for learning and enjoyment.

Kathy currently lives in San Antonio, Texas, with her cat, Cuddles. Her favorite activities involve teaching, writing, reading, fiber arts, and traveling.

Jenny C. Wilson is an associate professor of literacy at Texas A&M University, San Antonio, where she works with preservice and in-service teachers. Having been a teacher herself, she had many questions about teaching reading and writing, and she spent seven years at the University of Texas at Austin studying and working in those areas until achieving her MEd and PhD in 2007. While there, she taught fourth, seventh, and eighth grades and became a reading specialist and master reading teacher. In her seventeen years working with college students, she has taught classes in writing, assessment, theory, early and later-grade reading, and adolescent psychology and has facilitated preservice teachers. She loves it all!

She is interested in writing as storytelling within cultures in Liberia, and she travels there often to learn and study with schools that are attempting to make literacy possible. She also studies play as an impetus for storytelling and, of course, writing workshop for after-school programs and struggling writers and readers.

Jenny currently lives in San Antonio, Texas, with her two schnauzer mixes, Zoey and Charlie. Her favorite activities are journal writing, reading, and hiking.